Guidelines for Photocopying Reproducible Pages

Gospel Light's
baby beginnings

teacher's guide

0 to 18 months

Editorial Staff
Senior Managing Editor, Sheryl Haystead • **Senior Editor,** Debbie Barber • **Editorial Team,** Janis Halverson, Lisa Key, Nicole Silver • **Art Director,** Lenndy Pollard • **Designer,** Annette M. Chavez

Founder, Dr. Henrietta Mears • **Publisher,** William T. Greig • **Senior Consulting Publisher,** Dr. Elmer L. Towns • **Senior Consulting Editor,** Wesley Haystead, M.S.Ed.

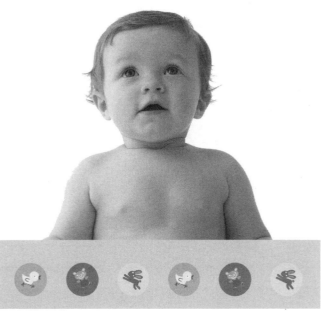

Gospel Light

CONTENTS

CD-ROM Parent's Home Pages

Parent's Home Pages—0 to 18 Months
Introductory Parent's Home Page

Year 1	Year 2
September	September
October	October
November	November
December	December
January	January
February	February
March	March
April	April
May	May
June	June
July	July
August	August

If You Are the Children's Pastor or Nursery Coordinator

• Prior to the start of each month, send home the appropriate month's overview (first two pages of each month's section) to each caregiver in the nursery.

• If you have a regular, consistent staff for the month, include the activity pages for the month as well and encourage your staff to plan together which activities they will prepare and provide each week of the month. (For example, one person would be prepared to lead a God's Wonders activity each week while another person would be prepared to lead an Active Play activity each week.)

• If you have a rotating staff, select several of the activities yourself. Collect any needed supplies and place them in the appropriate rooms along with the page of instructions (highlight or mark the activity). Alert the staff to look for these items when they arrive to serve.

Note: Consider creating for each room a box for each month that contains the supplies for the month's learning activities as described in the *Baby Beginnings Teacher's Guides*. At the beginning of the month, the box is placed in the appropriate rooms for use by teachers.

If You Are a Caregiver in the Nursery

For each month, select the activities you will provide. Collect needed supplies.

For Parents

• Distribute a copy of the reproducible *I Love to Sing!* CD to each family.

• At the beginning of each month, send home (or ask your children's pastor to send home) both the appropriate month's *I Love to Look!* Bible Story Picture Card and *Parent's Home Page*. *Parent's Home Pages* are available on the CD-ROM that comes with this book, as well as in *Nursery Smart Pages*. Purchase one set of *I Love to Look!* Bible Story Picture Cards for each family.

What Are They Like?

When we say "baby," we may mean a newborn. Or we may be referring to a sitter or to the crawler who picks up, inspects and eats every crumb! Although babyhood is short, the changes from newborn to toddler are enormous!

A newborn is quite aware of and sensitive to surroundings (especially the emotional "feel" of those surroundings), but sleeping and eating are the order of the day.

Around six weeks of age, a baby begins to reach out to touch items that interest him or her and to control his or her head.

A baby may become a sitter at around six months of age. Now that the baby's range of vision is broadened, he or she loves to reach (and perhaps even roll after) small objects, and drop, throw or bang them.

The crawler is now able to explore a brave new world! From the coffee cup to the full wastebasket, there is nothing that doesn't interest him or her. Once crawling is mastered, expect lots of pulling up, standing and attempts at climbing.

How Can I Help Them?

Position colorful mobiles hung so babies can see them. An occasional change of scenery and the gentle talking, rocking and comforting that accompany feeding, changing and sleep preparation should keep them happy and content. Be sure to support the head of a baby this age, even if he or she appears to have good control. Remember that frequent burping is necessary when feeding a newborn.

Give babies some time in positions other than the one in which they usually sleep. As a baby becomes able to roll over, he or she will be ready for more changes of scenery and more play and conversation with adults. An infant seat or other device that puts the baby where he or she can see what's going on nearby is helpful.

Once a baby can sit up, try playing peekaboo with him or her, or pushing gently on the baby's feet so the child can push back. Provide a number of safe smaller toys (rattles, fabric or vinyl blocks) and other objects for discovering. As you interact with a baby, describe his or her actions or responses to your actions.

For the crawler, freedom to explore within safe limits is the key. Provide lots of space for crawlers to roam without hazards. Crib mattresses and washable, firm pillows can provide a variety of safe crawling, climbing and sitting surfaces. Carpet-sample squares can provide interesting textures to crawl across. Your calm and happy interaction with babies on the floor helps them learn ways to explore and communicate.

A Smooth Schedule

There should be at least one caregiver for every three babies. This makes it possible to keep a close eye on every child's safety, as well as to give each child individual attention. If possible, the same caregiver should care for the same children from week to week. This continuity is especially important when babies begin to distinguish between strangers and friends!

When a baby arrives, give child and parents a friendly greeting! After check-in is complete, take a moment to talk to and sing to the child. To interest older babies in an activity, begin to do the activity yourself.

When it's time to change or move a child, don't pick up the child without warning; rather, talk calmly to him or her about what's going to happen. Never underestimate the power of your calmness and relaxed attitude. It will likely "rub off" onto the babies you care for!

Remember to watch, ask, and adapt yourself to the children's changing interests and activities. Your enthusiasm for the theme-related activities suggested in this guide and your interest in each child are what make this a time of effective learning.

"Get serious," some may say. "We're dealing with babies here. They just need to be fed, changed, rocked—what can they possibly learn about God?"

The Style in Which It's Done

While no one thinks it's vital to post charts of major theological concepts on the nursery wall, it is vital to think about what babies can learn. The goal of teaching in the nursery is not to get a baby to say, "God!" Rather, our goal is to individually (one-on-one) teach the baby what he or she can learn about God's love.

Such teaching is done by your every look, word and act while you are in the presence of a baby or toddler. You represent Christ to each little person in your care. Using a curriculum with monthly themes will help bring consistency to your efforts to help little ones learn about God.

What do you communicate to that baby who seems to throw up on you every time you hold him or her? Do you tense as you pick up the child, steeling yourself against the inevitable? That baby senses your tension! A baby is very sensitive to even such subtle things. And it tells the child how you feel about him or her! Conversely, when your words, looks and actions are relaxed and gentle, loving and kind, you teach the baby not only that people at the church nursery can be trusted, you are also building a foundation for that little child's trust in God!

The attitude in which you meet a baby's needs greatly influences his or her developing personality. As a baby associates you with pleasant experiences and lovingly having his or her needs met, he or she also forms foundational opinions about trusting and about being loved that will affect his or her whole life. This is why it is important, whenever possible, to care for the same babies each time you are in the nursery. Continuity of care means the baby becomes familiar with one person, building the baby's trust and comfort.

Talking with babies and toddlers about God and Jesus is a reminder to yourself of your purpose in serving in the nursery. Your example in ministering to these little ones will help parents begin to develop these same skills in communicating spiritual truths to their children.

Individual Time with Babies

Play simple games lovingly with babies (such as gently pedaling a baby's legs and saying, "Jesse, God made your strong legs!"). Sing short, simple songs about God's love to even the youngest baby.

Remember that no baby cares about your vocal quality! Your low, gentle song relaxes, calms and teaches trust. As a baby often hears his or her name associated with God's love, he or she begins to associate song, self, God and love. No, it won't turn out a pint-sized theologian. But these experiences build a foundation for faith in the perfect Father who loves His little ones.

Time for Toddlers

Toddlers will enjoy hearing brief Bible stories and verses and short, simple songs about God and Jesus. Use toddlers' names often and show you enjoy them. Repeated, short, direct sentences are often or quite well-understood by toddlers even if they don't make any verbal response.

Older babies and toddlers also enjoy looking at books with you. (Books for babies and toddlers need mainly pictures, not words.) With a picture book and a toddler in your lap, you are in position to look at the pictures and talk with the child about the pictures in the books. "Look, Elisa! There's a big, red apple. I like to eat apples. God made apples for us to eat."

Whether you interact with babies or toddlers, remember that letting God's love flow through you to each child is what makes your teaching in the nursery far more than just a "baby-sitting" experience!

"Babies and toddlers simply need to be fed, changed and played with . . . why would we need curriculum for them?"

First of all, our goal in using curriculum is not to get a baby to spout theological concepts! Instead, our goal is to individually (one-on-one) teach each baby through natural learning processes what he or she can begin to learn about God. Curriculum is designed to help you, the teacher, use the time you spend at church with little ones to build spiritual foundations.

Secondly, using curriculum also benefits you, the teacher, as much as the child. Singing and talking about Jesus is a powerful reminder that what you are doing is not just custodial care, but ministry in its truest sense. The same is true for parents. Babies and toddlers may not NEED to hear about Jesus, but parents DO need to begin talking comfortably about Him with their child. The model the church provides of how we care for and "teach" babies and toddlers is intended to help parents catch on to the fact that they can and should do the same things at home.

Curriculum provides you with ideas and words that help make your natural teaching effective. Since the best kind of teaching for babies and toddlers is primarily one-on-one, don't expect that these little ones will sit in a circle or have a group time, or even remain interested in what you are doing for very long. But as you sit on the floor talking and playing with two or three babies, make frequent use of the conversation ideas and songs suggested in this guide. Plan to provide several of the learning activities. Play portions of the CD, repeating the same songs frequently. The sounds, words, actions and most of all, the feelings that are created in this casual setting will flow into a natural pattern of teaching and learning that will eventually build a young child's understanding of God, Jesus and the loving comfort found in the people around him or her at church. And using a curriculum with monthly themes helps provide continuity to the activities in the nursery, especially when teachers change frequently.

In a large classroom where there are many children and adults in the same room, designate certain learning activities for each adult to provide for children throughout the session. For example, one teacher may position him- or herself on the floor near several books, looking and talking about them with interested children. Another adult may sit near an open area of the room with a container of rhythm instruments, playing them and singing songs with children in that area of the room. However, as the session progresses, adults need to be ready to move to "where the action is." Flexibility is key.

A baby's learning takes place all the time, as a natural part of living. So the teaching in your nursery is accomplished by your every look, word and act while you are in the presence of babies and toddlers. The nursery is ministry just as surely as teaching a theology class for adults would be. A nursery curriculum helps you to focus your playing, talking, caregiving, singing and finger plays in ways that familiarize a child with God's name and His love. Awareness of God's love for each child takes your time in the nursery far beyond the level of just singing "Itsy-Bitsy Spider" again!

What Is Discipline?

First, it is imperative to understand that "discipline" at any age level is not "punishment for bad behavior." Instead, the very word discipline means "teaching"—the very kind of teaching Jesus did with His disciples! Discipline is a door of opportunity: opportunity to teach children appropriate ways to meet their needs. Such teaching of these ways will be twofold: first, to immediately stop inappropriate behavior (behavior that might hurt a child, destroy materials or disrupt the group); second, to help the child find another, more appropriate way to behave.

Discipline of babies and toddlers should NEVER include any sort of negative physical touching (spanking, slapping, swatting, tapping, shaking, pulling, biting back, or the like). It also NEVER includes ridicule, sarcasm, threats or withholding any sort of care from a child.

Meeting Their Needs

Young children have a very small understanding of how the world works.

They have no idea of the consequences of their acts or how another child will respond to them. Part of the process of discipline is to help a child make sense of things even as you help the child understand appropriate ways to act. To meet the needs of very young children:

1. Prevent Problems. Be sure the environment is set up to be safe and "trouble-free." Young children need to be able to explore with as little restraint as possible; this helps a child develop his or her own internal controls and reduces stress on babies and adults alike. Also, having several identical toys can help when toddlers both want the same toy. Because toddlers are still too young to understand sharing, offering an identical toy can often avoid conflict.

2. Set Clear Limits. Use the word "no" as little as possible because it does not teach the child an appropriate way to act. Instead, give clear information about the situation. For example, "The truck is for rolling. We don't hit Jeremiah with it.

It will hurt him. The truck rolls on the floor. See?" Save use of the word "no" for dangerous situations in which the child must be immediately restrained.

3. Redirect Behavior. "Let's roll the truck. Look! I roll the truck to you. Can you roll it back to me?" Or offer another activity. "Here is a ball. We can roll the ball. Or you may roll the car. Jeremiah will roll the truck." Redirecting behavior does not mean trying to get a toddler to share or to apologize. This only results in adult frustration and toddler confusion! While your modeling of sharing and apologizing is an important part of your teaching, don't expect that toddlers will understand it—or imitate it—just yet!

4. Offer a Choice. When you offer, "You may play with the bear or the doll. Which one do you want?" you are giving the child a choice between two acceptable alternatives. You will often find that even the most resistant toddler is easily redirected!

5. Acknowledge Feelings. Use the words, "I see . . ." often. "Dana, I see you bumped your knee. You feel sad." Acknowledging what you see shows the child you understand and helps the child begin to make sense of his or her emotions.

6. Talk Through Problems. If you are "talking through" as you watch children (describing what you see and how children are reacting), you are already in the perfect position to help solve any problem situation going on. "Ryan wants the car. Janna wants the car. What can we do? Here is another car. Here is a truck. Which one would you like, Ryan?"

Of course, the most important part of this opportunity to teach is found in the way you behave! As you model caring and respectful behavior and follow the above guidelines to meet children's needs in appropriate ways, you will find not only that the nursery is more peaceful, but also that you are naturally helping children make sense of their world and solve their own problems. This also shows children that their caregivers are loving and considerate people who want to help them. And that is the essence of showing God's love to little ones!

It's a familiar scenario: a parent, hurrying to get into the church service on time, hands a baby to you. At that moment, the baby begins to scream! You are in the nursery to minister not only to babies but their families as well. What can you do to improve the situation?

Time to Separate

By around six or seven months, babies begin to very clearly distinguish who they know well and who is a stranger. In most children, this brings on a mild anxiety that is fairly easily dealt with by your gentle smiles and a few distractions. But some children appear to have feelings of screaming panic that just won't quit!

Always remember (and gently remind parents) that when a child cries at separation time, it is normal. It is part of the child's growing ability to distinguish between parents and strangers (and to prefer parents!). Your calm reassurance of both parents and child will make the separation easier all around. Help both child and parents know that you recognize and accept their feelings.

Acknowledge Feelings

Always encourage a parent to say a brief good-bye before leaving the nursery, telling the child that he or she will return: "I'll be back after you've played with toys for awhile." Then be ready to help the child become involved in an interesting activity. When good-bye routines are established, children and parents get to know what to expect, and separation should become less difficult.

Also, expect that a baby's anxiety may vary from week to week. Just when it seems that little Zack is comfortable with separation, he'll "slide back" into anxiety. Remember that this, too, is not a failure on anyone's part! It's simply a normal part of a baby's growth and is best dealt with calmly.

For most children, the crying will not last for long (although it may seem like a long time to you!). Usually, the child will soon calm down and become absorbed in an activity. But remember that you communicate love, relaxation and comfort by your words, your voice and your relaxed body posture, patting or stroking. If you are relaxed, the baby will likely follow your lead.

Crying It Out

Babies have legitimate reasons to cry! Don't leave them alone to "cry it out"—this sends the opposite message from what you want the child to remember. Because babies often have little experience with adults other than parents and little memory about past experience, it's legitimate for them to wonder if their parents are ever going to return!

Tips to Try

• Sing the same welcoming song every week or use other "welcoming rituals." It's also helpful for the same person to greet the child and settle him or her into the new surroundings each time.

• For some children, too much contact too soon with a stranger results in more fear. Take time instead to talk further with the parent so the child sees that the parent trusts and accepts you. With children who are obviously frightened by your attention, try indirect interaction, playing with a toy that interests a child and talking to the toy to draw the child's interest.

• If the child cries for an extended period of time, send for a parent. Many churches have a "crying policy" limiting how long a baby may cry before parents are summoned (usually about five minutes).

• Try blowing bubbles. Most babies find bubbles fascinating! Taking a baby outdoors briefly may have the same effect.

• Invite the parent to stay in the nursery for a while. If the parent stays, try having him or her leave for five minutes, then come back. Increase the length of time with each absence until the child (and parent) are comfortable.

• Invite families of infants who are having difficulty separating from parents to visit the room when no other children are present. Familiarity with the room can boost the child's comfort level.

September
I See God's Love at Church

Jesus Came to Church
(See Luke 2:22-38.)

"I like to come to church."
(See Psalm 122:1.)

This month you will help each child:

- feel secure and comfortable at church as you demonstrate God's love to the child;
- begin to associate God and Jesus with loving people and enjoyable activities.

Devotional

As you watch and learn from the babies and toddlers you teach, notice how anxious each one is for food to satisfy the pangs of hunger. No substitute will do! You may try bouncing and tickling, rocking and caressing, but a little one's crying will not stop until physical hunger is satisfied. This is one time when the child knows exactly what he or she needs.

Read 1 Peter 2:1-3. The apostle Peter urges us to have the same single-minded drive in satisfying our spiritual needs. Unfortunately, we often allow ourselves to be sidetracked. We try a wide variety of ways to find fulfillment or to eliminate problems. But our spiritual hunger continues, often making us as cranky as a hungry baby! Peter tells us that only the pure milk of the word (see verse 2) can nourish the deepest needs of the human soul. Take time to be fed. Recognize the symptoms of your need and satisfy that hunger!

As a teacher, the gentle care you provide young children introduces them to the nurture and love of the people who love God and His Son, the Lord Jesus. Your tasks may seem to involve only the physical care of changing, feeding, playing, cuddling and singing. However, those actions must be bathed in the warmth of Jesus' love. Such love will radiate from you as you take time each day to "taste" the goodness of the Lord (see Psalm 34:8). Just as babies single-mindedly demand to be fed, demand "time out" from your busy schedule to feed your soul from God's abundant resources.

During the month of September, display this poster at child's eye level. Talk about the way in which the children in the poster are experiencing God's love at church by playing with toys and friends.

I See God's Love at Church

Do It!

I Come In

I come in,
there's a smile on my face.
I come in,
my friends are in this place.
I come in,
my friends say "hi" to me.
I'm in church,
what a happy place to be!

Sing It!

It's Fun to Go to Church

(Tune: "Farmer in the Dell")

It's fun to go to church!
It's fun to go to church!
With all the other boys and girls
It's fun to go to church!

Tell It!

Jesus Came to Church

When Jesus was a baby,
His parents brought Him to church.
People at church were
glad to see baby Jesus.
They talked to Him.
They smiled at Him.
They held Him close.
Jesus was happy to be at church.
You can be happy at church
Because people show God's
love to you here.
(See Luke 2:22-38.)

Display this poster at teacher's eye level in your nursery. Tell the Bible story, sing the song, do the finger play and repeat the Bible verse to one or more interested children.

10 ● *Baby Beginnings® Teacher's Guide—0 to 18 Months*

Activities with Babies

Choose one or more of these learning activities to provide for babies during a session. Consider your facility, the number of babies and teachers and the supplies you have available as you plan which activities you will use. Continue the activity as long as the child is interested. For more information on using this curriculum, see "Why Use Curriculum?" on page 6.

Active Play

Who's in the Mirror?

Collect
Unbreakable hand mirror

Do
Hold a hand mirror so the child can see his or her face, then hands. Talk about and gently touch each part of the child's face while child looks in the mirror.

Say
Becca, God made your nose. God made you. God loves you!
I'm glad you came to church today. Thank You, God, for Becca.

Movement

What a Kick!

Collect
One or more washable stuffed animals

Do
Hold a pillow or soft toy above the baby's feet for the baby to kick.

Say
God loves you and He made your legs. It's fun to kick and play!
You play at home and you play when you go to church.

Music

Shakers

Collect
I Love to Sing! CD and player
Toy that makes noise when moved or a rhythm instrument such as a shaker

Do
Shake the toy or instrument, saying "Shake, shake, shake."
Let the baby try shaking the toy.
Play "A Happy Place" while you are playing with the baby. Shake one of the toys or instruments to the rhythm of the music.

Say
I'm glad you are happy.
God loves you.

My Church Song

Collect
I Love to Sing! CD and player

Do
Play and/or sing "Together" to babies as you rock, feed or play with them.

Say
Adriana, I'm so glad you are here today. We're glad to be at church with our friends.
God loves you.
Tip
Babies like to hear the same song over and over.

Pictures and Books

Families at Church

Collect

September Bible Story Picture from *I Love to Look!* or *Nursery Posters*

One or more sturdy books picturing families

Do

Hold a baby while looking at the pictures. If baby is interested, talk about families coming to church.

Point to and name each family member pictured. Relate the baby and his or her family to the people in the picture.

Say

This is a picture of Jesus. When Jesus was a baby, His parents brought Him to church.

Daniel, your dad brought you to church today. I'm glad you are here.

Madison, here's a picture of a big brother. You have a brother, too. You and your brother come to church. Thank You, God, for Madison and her brother.

Tip

Babies will want to explore the book with hands and mouths. Clean a book that has been in a baby's mouth.

Playing at Church

Collect

September Poster from *Nursery Posters* displayed at child's eye level

Do

Hold a baby in your arms or on your lap while you are near the photo and talk about the children in the photo.

Say

These children are playing with toys just like you play with toys at our church.

I'm glad you're here. God loves you and I do, too.

Quiet Play

The Cooing Game

Collect

Brightly colored toy

Do

Show a baby the toy. When the baby responds by cooing, imitate the baby's sound. Then give him or her a hug.

Continue imitating any other sounds the baby makes, smiling and nodding at the baby to encourage communication.

Say

I love you and God does, too!

Story Time

Do

Hold a baby in your lap, facing you. Say, "I'm going to tell you a story."

Tell a story about the baby coming to church. Use short sentences, pausing after each one to let the baby respond with coos or other sounds.

Say

I'm going to tell you a story.

Maria woke up today. Her mommy put her clothes on. Then Maria came to church with her mommy and daddy. At church, Maria played with the toys.

I like to tell you stories. It's fun to hear you talk. God loves you, Maria.

Activities with Toddlers

Choose one or more of the learning activities on pages 13-16 to provide for toddlers during a session. Consider your facility, the number of children and teachers and the supplies you have available as you plan which activities you will use. The best kind of teaching for toddlers will happen as you take advantage of teachable moments as children play and experience the learning activities you have provided. Continue an activity as long as one or more children are interested. For more information on using this curriculum, see "Why Use Curriculum?" on page 6.

Active Play

Build It!

Collect

Cardboard or wooden blocks

Do

Slowly build a tower, describing what you are doing and counting each block. Knock down the tower, or let child knock down the tower.

Encourage the child to build the tower again.

Say

I am putting one block on the floor. Now I'm putting another block on the floor. One, two. There are two blocks in our tower.

God made your hands. You can use your hands to play at home and at church.

Tip

While you are building a tower with a child, say, "Isaiah, you can only knock down your own tower. Eden gets to knock down the tower she built."

Copy Cats!

Do

Imitate a movement the child makes, or ask the child to wave or clap hands and then imitate the action.

Say

God made your hands and feet. I can see you are having fun waving and clapping.

It's fun to come to church. I'm glad you are here!

Teddy Bear

Collect

Two teddy bears (or other washable stuffed animals)

Do

Give a toddler a teddy bear and hold one yourself.

Act out the words of this poem with your teddy bear.

Teddy Bear, Turn Around

Teddy bear, teddy bear, turn around.
Teddy bear, teddy bear, touch the ground.
Teddy bear, teddy bear, I'll hug you tight.
Teddy bear, teddy bear, say "goodnight!"

Say

God loves you! God made your arms to hug your teddy bear.

Empty and Full

Collect

Two large containers (boxes, dishpans, etc.)
Small toys (too large to swallow) or blocks

Do

Children move toys from one container to the other. If the child empties a container say, "All gone! It's empty now!" Go to the other container and say, "It's full now."

Say

I'm glad you came to church today. God loves you!

Thank You, God, for loving Annie.

Art Play

Coloring Fun

Collect

Large sheets of white construction paper
Jumbo crayons

Do

Children color on paper. Identify the color of crayons child uses.

Say

Tyler, you're having fun drawing. I'm glad you like to draw.

God made your eyes to see these colors. God loves you. Thank You, God, for Your love.

Tip

If the child puts the crayon in his or her mouth, say, "Keep the crayon on the paper, not in your mouth."

Sticky Pictures

Collect

Large square of clear Con-Tact paper
Masking tape
2-inch (5-cm) colorful fabric and paper squares

Do

Tape Con-Tact paper (sticky side out) to wall at children's eye level. Invite children to attach fabric and paper squares to the sticky paper.

Say

Tyrell, you put a red paper on our sticky paper. It's fun to make a sticky picture.

I'm glad you came to help us make our sticky picture. God loves you.

God's Wonders

Mirror Fun

Collect

Unbreakable hand mirror

Do

Let each toddler have a chance to hold and look into the mirror. Talk about each part of the child's face.

Say

Can you see your brown eyes in the mirror? God made your eyes. God loves you.

I'm glad you're here today at our church.

What's in the Bag?

Collect

Fabric or paper bag
Variety of small child-safe items with different textures such as toy car, fabric ball, wooden block, etc.

Do

Place items inside bag. (It's OK if child sees you.) Invite child to put his or her hand in the bag and try to find one of the items. Talk about whichever item the child removes.

Say

What's in the bag, Zachary? You found the red block! Let's see if you can find some more toys in the bag.

I'm glad you came to church today to play with our toys. God loves you!

Music

Fun at Church

Collect

September Teaching Poster from *Nursery Posters*

Toys

Do

Move close to one or more children while they are playing with toys and begin to sing the song on the poster, substituting words describing what a child is doing. For example, if the child is playing with cars, sing "It's fun to play with cars."

Say

I'm glad Chino is having a good time at church today.

I like being with Chino at church. God loves you, Chino. Thank You, God, for Chino.

Together Actions

Collect

I Love to Sing! CD and player

Do

Play "Together" on CD. Sing along with the song, following along with the action suggested in the song. If children remain interested, substitute other actions for "make smiles" (wave hands, clap hands, etc.).

Say

We're so glad to be together today. I see Lily. I see Daniel. I see James.

We're having fun singing and smiling.

Pictures and Books

Books and Toys

Collect

September Poster from *Nursery Posters*

Several sturdy books that picture toys

Do

Take a book to where children are playing with toys. Compare the toys they have with the pictures in the book or the poster.

Say

It's fun to play with trucks. It's fun to come to church. I'm glad you are here.

Tip

Toys that are being ignored should be removed from sight to avoid clutter. Toddlers need open space more than they need a vast array of toys.

I Spy!

Collect

Several sturdy books that picture children

Do

Look at a book with a child. As you look at a page, say "I spy a girl who is playing with a doll." Ask the child to point to the girl and pause to see if child responds. If the child does not respond, point to the picture yourself. Repeat "I Spy!" activity as you continue to look through the book.

Say

It's fun to come to church and play with our friends. At church we learn that God loves us.

Pretend Play

Doll Play

Collect

One or more dolls or washable stuffed animals

Do

Give a toddler a doll or stuffed animal. Ask, "Where is the doll's head?" Repeat the question with other body parts: ears, legs, tummy, nose and eyes.

Suggest the child do specific things with the doll such as: feed the doll, tickle the doll's tummy, rock the doll, wrap the doll in a blanket.

Say

You're rocking the baby just like mommies and daddies rock their babies.

Mommies and daddies love their babies. God loves you, too.

Driving to Church

Collect

Several toy cars

Box or large block representing your church

Do

Sit on the floor with a child. "Drive" a car to the "church." Invite a child to drive a car to church, too. Talk about being glad to come to church.

Say

Let's pretend we're driving these cars to church. I'm glad to come to church. At church I hear that God loves me. God loves you, too, Emma. Thank You, God, for loving Emma.

I'm glad you are at church today.

Tip

Expect that children will use toy cars or other toys in a variety of ways. A toddler is likely to pretend to drive the car for a moment or two, and then wander off with the car to another area of the room. Be ready for teachable moments to use the suggested conversation.

Quiet Play

Match It!

Collect

Several toys with shapes that a toddler will recognize (book, block, car, etc.)
Paper
Jumbo crayons

Do

While child watches, trace around one toy on paper. Show the child how the toy and the shape match. An older toddler may be able to match the toy and shape by him- or herself.

Trace around several other toys, matching each toy to the shape. As children are interested, they match the toys and shapes and/or color on the shapes.

Say

We're playing with the toys. I like playing with you at church.

God loves you and so do I.

What's Hidden

Collect

Several large paper or plastic cups
Several toys (too large to be swallowed) that will fit inside the cups

Do

Place a cup over each toy. Give the child time to remove each of the cups.

Toddlers will want to repeat this game over and over again!

Say

God loves you. God made your hands. We are having fun using our hands.

When we come to church, we can play together. I'm glad you are here today.

October

Jesus Loves Children

Jesus Loved the Little Children
(See Mark 10:13-16.)

"Jesus loves the children."
(See Mark 10:16.)

• • • • • • • • • • • •

This month you will help each child:

• develop an awareness of the name of Jesus and associate Him with being loved;

• enjoy the activities provided.

Devotional

What does it mean to become like a child? How can an adult humble him- or herself to be childlike?

These questions must have gone through the minds of some of Jesus' disciples when He set a child in their midst in answer to their question about who is greatest. Read Matthew 18:1-4. This formula for greatness with the emphasis on little children sounded quite contrary to all the commonly accepted ideas about status. Perhaps as the disciples looked at the child Jesus had recruited for His object lesson, they began to see some of the qualities of the child that Jesus valued.

As you observe the babies and toddlers in your church, one of the first characteristics you may notice is their total dependence on others. Surely Jesus was calling attention to our dependence on

God. How often do we impair our effectiveness by thinking we can get by with just our own ability! What new horizons of growth might become visible to us if we could see beyond the limits of our own resources to what God has made available to us?

What other valuable childlike qualities can you nurture in your own life? Perhaps the openness of an infant should be cultivated? Might not the child's demonstrations of affection be good examples to imitate? What if adults showed a toddler's desire to learn? Carefully watch a child during the next session. Look for attributes in that child for you to imitate spiritually. It's the path to greatness!

During the month of October, display this poster at child's eye level. Talk about the child in the poster and Jesus' love for all children.

Do It!

Jesus Loves Us All

Who are the children Jesus loves?
Jesus loves us all!
He loves us when we clap;
He loves us when we crawl.
He loves us when we walk;
He loves us when we fall.
Who are the children Jesus loves?
Jesus loves us all.
Jesus loves you!

Sing It!

Each Little Child

(Tune: "Mary Had a Little Lamb")

Jesus loves each little child,
Little child, little child.
Jesus loves each little child,
He loves you, yes, He does.

Tell It!

Jesus Loved the Little Children

Jesus loved the little children.
Mommies and Daddies brought
their children to Jesus.
Jesus held the little babies close.
Big boys and girls walked to
Him all by themselves!
Jesus smiled at all the children.
And the children smiled at Him.
Some children came and sat near Jesus.
Some children climbed right up in His lap!
Jesus loved each one.
(See Mark 10:13-16.)

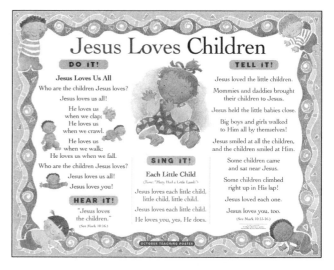

Display this poster at teacher's eye level in your nursery. Tell the Bible story, sing the song, do the finger play and repeat the Bible verse to one or more interested children.

Jesus Loves Children

Activities with Babies

Choose one or more of these learning activities to provide for babies during a session. Consider your facility, the number of babies and teachers and the supplies you have available as you plan which activities you will use. Continue the activity as long as the child is interested. For more information on using this curriculum, see "Why Use Curriculum?" on page 6.

God's Wonders

Pat the Pumpkin

Collect

One or two washed pumpkins of different sizes

Do

Place pumpkin on the floor or in the crib where a child can pat it.

Say

Michelle, you're touching the pumpkin. It's orange.

I'm glad you're here at our church today.

I love you, Michelle, Jesus loves you, too.

Movement

Push and Push

Do

Gently push your hands against a baby's feet while he or she is lying on a changing table or on a blanket on the floor. Talk about what the baby is doing and encourage his or her abilities.

Say

Caden, you are pushing with your feet. You are strong! Jesus loves you.

I'm glad to play with you.

Tip

Talk about other body parts the baby uses (hands, eyes). This activity will provide valuable stimulation for the baby's growing understanding of language.

Music

Softly Singing

Collect

I Love to Sing! CD and player

Do

Hold baby in a comfortable position. Gently rock or bounce the child as you play and/or sing "We're Special."

If the child shows enjoyment, try moving the child in more than one way (sway sideways, rock forward, etc.).

Say

It's fun to hold you and sing to you.

I love you, Xavier. Jesus loves you, too! Thank You, Jesus, for loving Xavier.

I Like to Wave!

Collect

I Love to Sing! CD and player

Do

Play "I Can Do" and follow the actions in the song, waving at a baby. Ask the baby to wave, too.

Say

Evan, can you wave your hand? I'm waving at you!

I'm glad to see you. I love you. Jesus loves you, too.

Pictures and Books

Jesus Loves Children

Collect

October Poster from *Nursery Posters*

One or more sturdy books picturing babies

Do

Hold a baby while looking at the poster or at pictures in the book. Talk about the children pictured as you point to them.

Say

Look at this boy sitting next to the pumpkin. This boy looks happy!

Jesus loves children. Jesus loves you!

Tip

If the baby responds with sounds, smile at the baby and respond by saying, "That's right! Jesus loves you, Skylar." Let the baby know you enjoy his or her responses.

Here Am I!

Collect

October Bible Story Picture from *I Love to Look!* or *Nursery Posters*

Photo album with pictures of each child (take pictures ahead of time to make a photo album to keep in your nursery)

Do

Hold or rock a child and look at pictures. Point to the picture of Jesus and talk about His love for children. Point to each child's picture and talk about His love for the child.

Say

Here is a picture of Jesus. Jesus loves children. Jesus loves you.

Meara, do you see your picture? Jesus loves you.

Quiet Play

Tap Your Toes

Do

Lay the baby in a crib or on a blanket on the floor. Talk to the baby, touching his or her hands and feet as you talk.

If the baby is interested in the attention, lightly tap the baby's hands and feet as you say:

Tap, tap, tap your toes.
Tap your fingers, too.
I like to play with you!

Say

I love to play with you, Jada. Jesus loves you!

Tip

Repeat the words and actions in the same way. The baby's enjoyment in the game will increase as he or she discovers what is coming next.

Toot, Toot, Toot!

Collect

Washable stuffed toy

Do

Place the baby on his or her back on a blanket.

Use the toy to gently nudge the baby on his or her hand, and then gently roll the stuffed toy over the baby saying:

Toot, toot, toot, here I come!
I'm going to roll-l-l-l over you.

Say

This bear is soft and fuzzy, Rachel.

It's fun to play together. Jesus loves us when we play. Jesus loves us all the time. Thank You, Jesus, for Your love.

Activities with Toddlers

Choose one or more of the learning activities on pages 21-24 to provide for toddlers during a session. Consider your facility, the number of children and teachers and the supplies you have available as you plan which activities you will use. The best kind of teaching for toddlers will happen as you take advantage of teachable moments as children play and experience the learning activities you have provided. Continue an activity as long as one or more children are interested. For more information on using this curriculum, see "Why Use Curriculum?" on page 6.

Active Play

Follow Me!

Do

Lead children in following you around the room: walking, running, crawling, stomping as desired.

Say

Some children went to see Jesus one day. Maybe they walked. Maybe they ran. Maybe they crawled.

Jesus was happy to see them. Jesus loves children. Jesus loves you. Thank You, Jesus, for loving James.

Roll the Ball

Collect

Several fabric or soft balls

Do

Roll the ball to a child as you say "Jesus loves Aiden."

Say

Jesus loves children. Jesus loves you.

We're having fun playing together.

I'm glad to know that Jesus loves us.

Tip

Toddlers do not usually play together or interact with each other in significant ways. Having more than one ball available will make it easy for you to involve several children in this activity.

Hide and Seek

Collect

Toy car or animal

Do

Hold the car or animal in your hand, showing it to a child. Then place the car behind a book or other object on a shelf. Ask the child to find the hidden object. The child may walk to where the toy is hidden and pull it out. If not, pretend to look in several places around the room. When you find the toy, say, "I found it!"

Say

Let's play a game. I'm going to hide this car. Where is the car? It's hiding! Let's find it.

It's fun to play hide and seek with you. Jesus loves us when we play. Jesus loves us all the time.

Travel Game

Collect

Blanket or towel

Doll or washable stuffed animal

Do

Put a doll or stuffed animal on the blanket or towel. Slowly pull it across the floor.

Pretend the "traveler" is riding in a car, train or airplane and make the appropriate sounds. A child may wish to pull the towel or blanket also and make the sounds.

Say

We can pretend we're riding in a train. Jesus loves us wherever we go!

Anthony, Jesus loves you.

Art Play

Happy Face Pictures

Collect

Paper plates
Jumbo crayons

Do

Before class, draw a simple happy face on each paper plate.
In class, children color faces.

Say

I see lots of happy faces! We're happy because Jesus loves us.
Jesus loves you, Bella. Jesus loves all the children.

Jesus Loves Children Picture

Collect

Magazine pictures of children
Glue sticks
Construction or drawing paper with "Jesus Loves Children" printed at the top

Do

Put glue on paper and help child place picture on the glue.

Say

These words say "Jesus Loves Children."
Which picture would you like to glue on this paper?
Jesus loves all children. Jesus loves you, Matthew.

God's Wonders

Touch and Feel

Collect

Several washed seasonal items (pumpkin, Indian corn, squash)

Do

With supervision, children look at and touch the items. Talk with children about the variety of textures and colors.

Say

Ben, this corn feels bumpy. You can touch the corn with your hands. Jesus loves you, Ben.

Tip

Place items on a tray that can be set out of children's reach when supervision is not possible.

Comparing Leaves

Collect

Variety of fall leaves placed on a tray

Do

Set tray of leaves where children can look at and touch them.

Say

Katelyn, here is a leaf that is red. Thank You, Jesus, for the leaves.
Jesus loves us. Jesus loves children.

Pictures and Books

Jesus Loves Me

Collect

October Bible Story Picture from *I Love to Look!* or *Nursery Posters*

Do

Show and talk about the picture. If a child is interested, tell the brief story printed on the back of the picture card.

Say

Here is a picture of Jesus. Jesus loves children. These children were glad to see Jesus.

Jesus loves you. I'm glad that Jesus loves us.

Tip

Some children will want to carry the picture card around or set it somewhere in the room. That's fine. After a child has lost interest in the picture card, pick up the card and show it to another child.

Pretend Play

Sound Off

Collect

Several toy farm animals

Do

Hand an animal to a toddler. Make the sound the animal makes several times. Ask the toddler to make the sound, too.

Say

Let's pretend to be sheep. What does a sheep say? As we walk around the room, let's say "baa, baa."

I'm glad you're having fun, Savannah. Jesus loves you!

Music

Music March

Collect

I Love to Sing! CD and player

Do

Play "Watch Me!" While music plays, march around the room and follow the actions suggested in the song. Children may also walk in a variety of ways: on tiptoe, jumping, sliding feet, crawling, etc.

Say

It's fun to play together. Jesus loves you when you play.

Jesus loves you all the time! Thank You, Jesus, for loving Carlos.

Drum Fun

Collect

One or two clean empty plastic containers; optional—*I Love to Sing!* CD and player

Do

Turn containers upside down. Use your hands, other toys and objects in the room to tap on the container like a drum. Encourage an interested child to follow your example. (Optional: Play "We're Special" as child taps on the drums.)

Say

I like making music with you!

Jesus loves you!

Quiet Play

Big or Small

Collect

Variety of big and small toys (large enough to prevent swallowing)

Do

Children play with toys. Talk about which toys are big and which are small.

Say

We're having fun playing with our toys. I see a big truck. And I see a small block.

Jerome, I'm glad you are here. Jesus loves you. Jesus loves all the children.

People Play

Collect

Small people figures too large to choke on

Do

Let children play with people freely.

Say

Mommies and daddies love their children. Jesus loves children, too. Jesus loves you. Thank You, Jesus, for Your love.

Wiggles

Do

Sit on the floor with a toddler. Say, "My thumbs are starting to wiggle round and round and round." Encourage the child to try these actions. Smile and nod your head when the child joins in.

Substitute other words such as "feet" and "hands." Use words that may be new or less familiar such as "elbows," "chin" or "shoulders" to continue the game.

Say

It's fun to play with you, Eric. Jesus loves you and I do, too.

Swing and Sway

Do

Invite a child to hold hands with you. Gently swing your hands and sway back and forth as you say the words "Jesus loves Aly." Repeat with other interested children.

Say

I like to talk about Jesus' love. Jesus loves you. Jesus loves all the children.

Tip

If a child is tired, hold him or her and gently sway or rock in a rocking chair while saying the words. If a child is full of energy, clap hands together while saying the words.

November

God Gives Me Food

Jesus Gave Food to His Friends
(See John 21:9-13.)

"God gives us food."
(See Genesis 1:29.)

This month you will help each child:
• develop an awareness that God made food;
• enjoy eating food with teachers and other children.

Devotional

After fishing all night, Jesus' disciples should have needed no coaxing to begin eating. Yet there they stood on the beach, dumbfounded that their Lord who had recently risen from the dead, made two miraculous appearances in locked rooms, and produced an abundant catch of fish from previously sterile water was now standing beside a fire, cooking their breakfast. Read John 21:9-13.

As the disciples stood there, Jesus served their food. He knew that His earthly ministry was quickly drawing to a close. He knew He must give great attention to preparing the disciples for their coming responsibility. Nevertheless, Jesus took time for a simple act of kindness to meet a basic physical need. When we meet the basic needs of babies and toddlers, we are a reflection of Jesus' kindness.

Have you recently recounted the needs in your life that Jesus has helped you meet? What problems has He helped you cope with successfully? What challenge has He helped you to meet? What burdens has He helped make lighter? And then, have you thanked Him for the many ways in which He has helped you? Scripture reminds us, "Do not be anxious about anything, but in everything, by prayer and petition, with thanksgiving, present your requests to God. And the peace of God, which transcends all understanding, will guard your hearts and your minds in Christ Jesus" (Philippians 4:6-7).

During the month of November, display this poster at child's eye level. Talk about the child in the poster and express thankfulness for the good food God helps us have.

Do It!
My Food

This is my nose
To smell my cracker.
These are my eyes
To see my cracker.
These are my hands
To hold my cracker.
This is my tongue
To taste my cracker.
Thank You, God,
For my cracker.

Tell It!
Jesus Gave Food to His Friends

Jesus' friends were hungry.
So Jesus cooked some fish and bread.
"Come and eat!" Jesus said.
The fish and bread tasted good.
Jesus' friends were glad He
gave them food.
We are glad for our food, too.
(See John 21:9-13.)

Sing It!
I Thank God

(Tune: "Mulberry Bush")

Apples taste so good to me,
So good to me, so good to me.
Apples taste so good to me.
I thank God for my food.

Display this poster at teacher's eye level in your nursery. Tell the Bible story, sing the song, do the finger play and repeat the Bible verse to one or more interested children.

Activities with Babies

Choose one or more of these learning activities to provide for babies during a session. Consider your facility, the number of babies and teachers and the supplies you have available as you plan which activities you will use. Continue the activity as long as the child is interested. For more information on using this curriculum, see "Why Use Curriculum?" on page 6.

God's Wonders

Fruity Colors

Collect

Several kinds of fruit (red and green apples, yellow pear, orange)

Do

Let children touch the various kinds of fruit. Identify the name and color of each fruit.

Say

Look at this red apple. Brendan, you are touching the red apple.

God made good food for us to eat. Thank You, God!

Movement

Catch the Toy

Collect

Several colorful toys

Do

Move a toy slowly in front of a baby. As the baby tracks the movement with his or her eyes or reaches for the toy, stop the movement so the baby can catch the toy. Repeat as long as child is interested, using several different toys.

Say

You caught the ball, Gabriella!

Thank You, God, for Gabriella. Thank You, God, for good food.

Music

Thank You

Collect

I Love to Sing! CD and player
Toy or real apple

Do

Play and sing along with "Thank You, God." Show apple and let baby touch it.

Say

I love to eat apples. God gives us such good food to eat!

Tip

Sing this song whenever you serve a snack to a child. He or she will enjoy the repetition and you will build a habit of thanking God for the way He provides for us.

I Like Food

Collect

I Love to Sing! CD and player
Variety of rhythm instruments

Do

Play "Food for Me." Play a rhythm instrument for a baby to hear. An older baby may be able to hold and move an instrument.

Say

I hear bells. I hear shakers.

We're singing about the good food God gives us.

Pictures and Books

Name the Food

Collect

Sturdy book picturing food and/or babies being fed

Do

Hold a baby and look at the book. Name the foods that are shown.

Say

Look at the good food in this book. I see some bread. I see some cheese. I see some juice.

God gives us good food to eat.

Friends Eat Together

Collect

November Bible Story Picture from *I Love to Look!* or *Nursery Posters*

Do

Show the picture to a baby. Talk about eating good food.

Say

Jesus ate with His friends. We like to eat with our friends at church, too.

God gives us good food to eat. We eat crackers and drink water with our friends at church.

Tip

A baby will show interest in a book by looking at it, touching it or making sounds. Continue looking at the book as long as the baby is interested.

Quiet Play

Hide It!

Note: Post a note alerting parents to the use of food. Also, check children's registration forms for possible food allergies.

Collect

Age-appropriate snack (banana slice, small cheese cube, Cheerios, etc.)

Paper napkins

Do

Place a baby who can sit up on the floor on a blanket. Place the snack between two napkins. Let the baby find the snack and eat it.

Repeat this game, letting the baby find the snack each time.

Say

Can you find the snack?

God made good food for us to eat. Thank You, God, for our food.

Snack Bowl

Note: Post a note alerting parents to the use of food. Also, check children's registration forms for possible food allergies.

Collect

Two kinds of age-appropriate crackers (or other snack)

Plastic bowl

Do

Hold the baby while seated at a child-sized table, or place a baby on the floor on a blanket. Offer the snack bowl to the baby. Watch to see if the baby prefers one snack over the other. Offer the child a little more of the preferred snack.

Say

You are eating a cracker, Marco! Marco likes the fish crackers.

God made crackers. He made your tongue to taste them.

Activities with Toddlers

Choose one or more of the learning activities on pages 29-32 to provide for toddlers during a session. Consider your facility, the number of children and teachers and the supplies you have available as you plan which activities you will use. The best kind of teaching for toddlers will happen as you take advantage of teachable moments as children play and experience the learning activities you have provided. Continue an activity as long as one or more children are interested. For more information on using this curriculum, see "Why Use Curriculum?" on page 6.

Active Play

Gathering Eggs

Collect
Several baskets with handles
Several dozen plastic eggs

Do
Place the eggs around the room.
Children find eggs and place them in baskets.

Say
God made chickens. Chickens give us eggs. God gives us good food.
I like to eat scrambled eggs. I'm glad God gives us good food to eat.
Thank You, God, for giving us food.

Snacking Game

Note: Post a note alerting parents to the use of food. Also, check children's registration forms for possible food allergies.

Collect
Masking tape
Plastic bowl
Age-appropriate snack (dry cereal, crackers, etc.)

Do
Before class, make two parallel masking-tape lines on the floor about 2 feet (.6 m) apart.
In class, place the bowl with the snack in it at one end of the lines. Invite a child to walk with

you between the lines toward the snack. Eat snack when you reach it. Repeat the activity with interested children.

Say
God made bananas that taste so good. I'm glad God gives us food.

Pouring

Note: Post a note alerting parents to the use of food. Also, check children's registration forms for possible food allergies.

Collect
Same-sized paper cups
Age-appropriate snack (dry cereal, crackers, etc.)
Tray

Do
Sit with a toddler at a child-sized table. Give the child two cups placed on a tray. Put a small amount of snack in one cup and show the child how to pour the snack into the other cup.
If the child is interested, give him or her plenty of time to explore pouring the snack back and forth before eating the snack.

Say
God made your hands so you can pour the cereal. God made your mouth so you can eat the cereal. I'm glad God gives us good food to eat.

Tip
A child masters skills by repeating an action again and again. The first time a child tries to pour the cereal, it will probably spill onto the tray. That's OK. Scoop up the spilled cereal, and let the child try again.

Active Play

Picnic Time

Collect

Paper bag or picnic basket
Blanket or towel
Toy food

Do

Put a few toy food items into a paper bag or picnic basket. Give child the bag or basket and lead him or her on a walk around the room.

Spread a blanket or towel on the floor and have a picnic, setting out and pretending to eat the toy food.

Say

I like to go on picnics. God helps us have good food to eat.

God's Wonders

Where Carrots Grow

Collect

Several whole carrots with tops still on

Do

Let children handle carrots and tops. Talk about where the carrot grew before it was picked.

Say

These carrots grew in the ground.
God gives us good food to eat. God loves you.

Music

I Like to Eat!

Collect

I Love to Sing! CD and player

Do

Play "Food for Me" for children. Clap along with the song and encourage children to clap, too.

Say

This song tells about the good food God gives us to eat. I'm so glad we have food to eat.

Tip

Even if singing is not your talent, toddlers enjoy hearing the rhythm and melody.

Thank You, God

Collect

I Love to Sing! CD and player
Several apples, bananas and oranges

Do

Play "Thank You" for children. Let children hold apples. Repeat song several times, substituting "bananas" and then "oranges" for the word "apples." Children hold appropriate items.

Say

Look at the food God gives for us to eat. I see an apple. I see an orange. I see a banana. Jordan, which one do you want to hold?

I like to eat apples. I'm glad God gives us good food to eat.

Art Play

Tablecloth

Collect

Pictures of food cut from magazines or grocery store ads, at least three or four for each child (Note: Pictures should be at least 2x3-inches [5x7.5-cm] in size.)
Glue sticks
Length of butcher paper taped to a child-sized table

Do

Show children how to put glue onto the paper and stick a picture on top of the glue. Children choose several pictures and glue them onto the paper.

Say

We're gluing pictures of food to make our tablecloth look pretty.

God gives us good food to eat because He loves us.

Pictures and Books

Fish Crackers

Note: Post a note alerting parents to the use of food. Also, check children's registration forms for possible food allergies.

Collect

November Bible Story Picture from *I Love to Look!* or *Nursery Posters*
Fish crackers

Do

Show and talk about the picture. Give children fish crackers to eat.

Say

Jesus cooked some food for His friends. They ate some bread and fish.

We have good food to eat, too. God made our food. God loves us.

Pretend Play

Feed Me!

Collect

Doll
Spoon
Paper cup

Do

Use the spoon and cup to pretend to feed the doll and give it something to drink. The child may imitate your actions. Talk about what kind of food you are feeding the doll.

Say

Your doll says, "Feed me, please. I'm hungry."
I like to eat lots of different kinds of food. What do you like to eat? What are you feeding your doll? Thank You, God, for our food.

I'm Eating Pancakes!

Do

Say the following words and do the appropriate motions, inviting a child to imitate your actions and pretend to make and eat pancakes.

Mix a pancake,
Stir a pancake,
Pop it in the pan.

Fry the pancake,
Toss the pancake—
Catch it if you can.

Say

God gives us good foods like pancakes to eat.

Telephone Talk

Collect

Play telephone

Do

Hold the telephone. Pretend to make the phone ring. Pick up the phone can carry on a conversation about what you like to eat. Then give the phone to the child so that he or she can talk to mom or dad. Watch to see if the child imitates your conversation.

Say

Hi! I like to eat applesauce and yogurt. What do you like to eat?

It's your mom. She wants to know what you like to eat.

I'm glad we have good food to eat. Thank You, God, for our food.

Tip

Talk frequently to children, describing their clothing and their actions. Long before a child can speak, he or she can grasp the meaning of words spoken or sung.

Quiet Play

Puzzles

Collect

Several puzzles with large, colorful pieces (if possible, provide at least one puzzle that shows food or sources of food)

Do

Talk about each picture in the puzzle. Let a toddler take out the puzzle pieces. Some children may be ready to attempt putting the pieces back in place.

Say

Chloe, you took out the puzzle piece of the apple. Apples taste good. I'm glad God made apples.

Damon, your puzzle shows a farm. I see some cows. God made cows so that we could have good milk to drink.

Tip

Help a toddler as needed by moving a puzzle piece close to where it fits, by turning a piece so it is almost in place, or by putting a piece in and letting the child take it out and replace.

Eggs in the Carton

Collect

Plastic eggs (enough for several children to each have two or three)

Several empty egg cartons (cut each carton in half)

Do

Children put plastic eggs in and out of the cartons. Talk about the good food God helps us have.

Say

Let's put these eggs into the cartons. I like to eat eggs. They taste good to me.

I'm glad that God loves us and gives us good food to eat.

Fruit Sort

Collect

Toy fruits in a variety of colors and sizes, at least two of each color

Do

Set out the fruits. Hold up one fruit and say its color. Ask a child to find a fruit of the same color. Repeat as long as the child is interested. You may also ask a child to point to the biggest, and then the smallest fruit.

Say

Joshua, I'm holding an orange. Can you point to another orange? That's right! Oranges taste so good! Thank You, God, for oranges.

God gives us good food to eat.

Cereal Box Towers

Collect

Variety of empty cereal boxes

Do

Set out cereal boxes and let an interested child stack them. Child may also set them up on a table or shelf. Count the boxes.

Say

Riley, do you like to eat cereal? God loves you and gives good food for you to eat.

Let's count the cereal boxes.

Tip

Counting aloud as you point to each cereal box will help toddlers begin to recognize numbers. Limit your counting to two or three boxes at a time.

December
Jesus Was a Baby

Jesus Was Born
(See Luke 2:4-7.)

"His name is Jesus."
(See Luke 1:31.)

• • • • • • • • • • •

This month you will help each child:

• show interest in activities, conversation and songs about baby Jesus;

• receive personal attention and love as teachers seek to show Jesus' love in ways a child understands.

Devotional

There was never a birth announcement to equal it! On a nearby hillside angels were proclaiming joy, salvation and peace. In a faraway land, a group of wise men were stunned by the appearance of a star.

Immediately after hearing the news, the shepherds rushed into Bethlehem; the wise men began to plan for their trek westward. The accounts in Luke and Matthew reflect great excitement and joy. Read the accounts of their journeys in Matthew 2:1-12 and Luke 2:4-20. But what followed the first flush of emotion, the awe and wonder of the event?

The shepherds returned to their hillside, continuing their daily rounds of herding the flocks. The wise men faced an arduous journey through strange and possibly dangerous lands. And Mary and Joseph faced the daily routines of caring for an infant. The excitement lasted only a short time, then the familiar patterns of normal life were re-sumed. But even though the angel choir was gone, "Mary treasured . . . all these things . . . in her heart" (Luke 2:19).

December may be filled with much excitement for your family and church. However, in the midst of the celebrations, take time to treasure the presence of Christ in daily living. Set aside moments to ponder the ways He touches your life with joy, salvation and peace.

During the month of December, display this poster at child's eye level. Talk about the items in the poster which remind us of Jesus' birth.

Do It!

Look into the Stable

Look into the stable now.
Who do you see?
I see baby Jesus sleeping
In Mary's arms.

Look into the stable now.
What do you hear?
I hear baby Jesus laughing
In Joseph's arms.

Sing It!

Happy Birthday, Jesus!

(Tune: "Jesus Loves Me")

It's Jesus' birthday, time to sing!
Shake the bells and make them ring.
Let's all sing a happy song.
Bring your drums and march along.

Happy birthday, Jesus,
Happy birthday, Jesus,
Happy birthday, Jesus.
We sing this happy song.

Tell It!

Jesus Was Born

Mary held her baby.
Her baby's name was Jesus.
She rocked Him gently in her arms
And sang a quiet song to Him.
Joseph held baby Jesus
And watched Him wiggle and laugh.
All through every day, and
all through every night,
Mary and Joseph loved and
cared for baby Jesus.
We are glad baby Jesus was born.
(See Luke 2:4-7.)

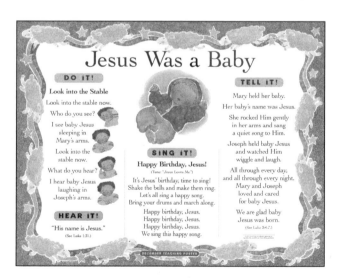

Display this poster at teacher's eye level in your nursery. Tell the Bible story, sing the song, do the finger play and repeat the Bible verse to one or more interested children.

Activities with Babies

Choose one or more of these learning activities to provide for babies during a session. Consider your facility, the number of babies and teachers and the supplies you have available as you plan which activities you will use. Continue the activity as long as the child is interested. For more information on using this curriculum, see "Why Use Curriculum?" on page 6.

Active Play

Touch and Feel

Collect

One or more of these items for babies to touch (soft blanket, pitch-free pinecones without sharp points, Christmas greenery such as a pine branch)

Do

With supervision, let babies look and touch items you collected.

Say

This blanket is soft. We wrap babies in soft blankets. Jesus was a baby. We're glad He was born.

Olivia, you are touching the pinecone and the branches. They feel hard. God made your hands.

Movement

Jingle Bells

Collect

Securely fasten several large jingle bells to a thick length of yarn

Do

Hold the yarn near a baby's hands or feet. Each pull or kick on the yarn will reward him or her with an instant and cheerful ringing.

Say

Do you hear the bells? I like the sound of happy bells. We're happy because Jesus was born.

Thank You, God, for Jesus.

Music

Ring Those Bells

Collect

Bell or other rhythm instruments

Do

While holding a baby, show the baby the bell or other rhythm instrument. Ring the bell or play the instrument. Lightly bounce the baby and make the bell ring.

Say

This music makes me glad. I'm glad Jesus was born.

Christmas Carol

Collect

I Love to Sing! CD and player

Do

Play "Christmas Party" while you hold or play with a baby.

Say

I like to sing about Jesus. Jesus was a baby. We're glad Jesus was born.

Tip

Play music at a low volume to help create a cheerful, welcoming atmosphere. Sing or hum along with the songs. Babies will enjoy and respond to the sound of your voice.

Pictures and Books

Baby Books

Collect

December Bible Story Picture from *I Love to Look!* or *Nursery Posters*

Sturdy books picturing babies and families

Do

Hold a baby in your lap to look at a book or the picture. Describe what you see.

Say

Look at this baby. She is holding a ball.

Jesus was a baby. This picture shows Jesus when He was a baby. We are thankful that Jesus was born.

Sleepy Baby

Collect

December Poster from *Nursery Posters* displayed at child's eye level

Do

Talk about the photo with a child. Point to and identify the facial features (eyes, nose, mouth, fingers) of the baby in the photo.

Say

See the baby? The baby is sleeping. Her eyes are closed. There is her mouth. There is her nose. Jesus was a baby.

Quiet Play

Christmas Toys

Collect

Several child-safe colorful fabric Christmas ornaments

Do

Place ornaments in a baby's crib, or on the floor while baby is lying on a blanket. Talk about the ornaments to the baby.

Say

Look at the star. It's yellow. And I see a red bell. The star and the bell remind us of Jesus' birthday. Jesus was a baby.

Tip

The baby may not understand most of your words, but he or she will enjoy the sounds and rhythm of your voice and the special attention.

Rolling Toy

Collect

Rolling toy that makes noise when it moves

Do

Near the baby's head, hold a rolling toy that makes noise when it moves. Tap the toy. When the baby looks at the toy, roll it a short distance. Then put the toy back by the baby's head. Repeat the activity, commenting on the baby's actions.

Say

I'm glad to play with you, Abby. When Jesus was a baby, His mommy and daddy played with Him.

I'm glad Jesus was born. Thank You, God, for Jesus.

Activities with Toddlers

Choose one or more of the learning activities on pages 37-40 to provide for toddlers during a session. Consider your facility, the number of children and teachers and the supplies you have available as you plan which activities you will use. The best kind of teaching for toddlers will happen as you take advantage of teachable moments as children play and experience the learning activities you have provided. Continue an activity as long as one or more children are interested. For more information on using this curriculum, see "Why Use Curriculum?" on page 6.

Active Play

Christmas Shopping

Collect

Several gift bags (with handles, if possible)
Christmas items (stuffed fabric ornaments, bows, pieces of wrapping paper, Christmas cards)

Do

Set Christmas items on floor or child-sized table. Give an interested child a bag. Ask, "What are you going to put in your bag?" When a child puts an item into the bag, name and describe the item.

Say

Paloma, you put a big red bow in your bag. Marcus, you put a picture of angels in your bag.
We're glad that it is Jesus' birthday! Jesus was a baby. We love Jesus!

Tip

Often when one child is playing with an item, other children will want to participate. Have several duplicate items ready to hand out.

Walking to Bethlehem

Do

Take children for a walk around the room.

Say

Let's pretend we are walking to Bethlehem, like Mary and Joseph. Jesus was born in Bethlehem. Mary was Jesus' mother.
I'm glad Jesus was born. Thank You, God, for Jesus.

Find the Nativity Scene

Collect

Child-safe nativity scene

Do

Show children the nativity scene figures. Then hide the figures in different places around the room, accessible to children. (It's OK if children watch where you hide them.)

Say

Can you find the shepherd in our room? The shepherds went to see baby Jesus. The shepherds loved Jesus. We love Jesus, too.
I'm glad Jesus was born!

Build a Barn

Collect

Cardboard blocks
Toy animals

Do

Build a barn with the blocks. Hold up an animal and say its name. Let a child hold the animal or put it in the barn. Continue playing with the blocks and animals as long as the children are interested.

Say

Jesus was born a long time ago. He was born in a barn where animals sleep and eat.
We're glad Jesus was born.

Art Play

Christmas Pictures

Collect

9x12-inch (23x30.5-cm) sheet of red, green or white construction paper for each child
Seasonal stickers

Do

Each child chooses a paper. Help children put stickers on paper any way they choose.

Name the items as they are placed on the paper.

Say

This is a sheep. Sheep live in barns. Jesus was born in a barn called a stable. I'm glad Jesus was born.

Joshua, you are putting your stickers on a red paper. I see lots of star stickers on your paper. There was a special star in the sky when Jesus was born.

Ornaments on the Tree

Collect

One or more large Christmas trees cut from green paper
Masking tape
Large round circle stickers or other seasonal stickers

Do

Tape tree to wall at children's eye level.

Children put ornaments on the tree by attaching the stickers.

Say

Let's decorate our Christmas tree. We're happy because Jesus was born.

We love Jesus.

God's Wonders

Decorations

Collect

Several pinecones and fresh evergreen boughs (no poisonous plants such as poinsettia and holly berries)

Do

Set pinecones and greenery on a child-sized table or shelf where toddlers can see and touch them. Invite children to smell the evergreen boughs.

Say

We put branches like these and pinecones in our church. We want our church to look pretty to show how happy we are that baby Jesus was born.

Thank You, God, for baby Jesus.

Tip

Store items out of reach when you are unable to closely supervise children's play with them.

Do You Feel What I Feel?

Collect

Soft blanket
Hay or straw (may be purchased at craft store)
Fake lamb's wool

Do

Set out items on table or tray on the floor. Children who are interested touch and hold items. Talk about Jesus' birth.

Say

Nicholas, can you feel how soft this blanket is? Moms and dads wrap their babies in soft blankets. Jesus was a baby. We're glad He was born.

Jesus was born in a barn. Sheep sometimes live in a barn, too. Can you feel this wool?

Music

Play It!

Collect

I Love to Sing! CD and player
Small blocks

Do

Sit with a toddler and tap two blocks together to make a sound. Play "Christmas Party" while you tap the blocks together.

Hand two blocks to the child to tap together.

Say

We're singing happy music because we're glad Jesus was born.

Thank You, God, for Jesus.

Pictures and Books

Where's the Picture?

Collect

December Bible Story Picture from *I Love to Look!* or *Nursery Posters*
Sturdy books picturing Mary, Joseph and baby Jesus
Sheet of paper

Do

Show the picture or book to a child. Talk about the pictures. Point to the picture of Jesus and ask the child to point to it, too.

Hold a sheet of paper over a picture, asking "Where is the picture of baby Jesus?" Then remove the paper and say, "There it is. There's baby Jesus!"

Say

I see a picture of Jesus' mommy. Her name was Mary. Can you point to the picture of Mary?

Jesus was a little baby once. We're glad Jesus was born. Where's the picture of Jesus?

Pretend Play

Animals in the Barn

Collect

Toy farm animals
Blocks

Do

Sit on the floor with a toddler, giving him or her several toy farm animals. Outline a barn with blocks.

One at a time put the animals into the barn, making the sound of each animal. An interested child will put animals in and take them out of the barn and make the animal sounds.

Say

Anthony, you put the cow into the barn. What does a cow say? Moo.

These animals live in a barn. Jesus was born in a barn. We're glad Jesus was a baby.

Baby Doll

Collect

Dolls
Doll blankets

Do

Give a toddler a doll and a blanket. Hold a doll and blanket yourself. Put the blanket around the doll and let the child imitate you. Pretend to rock, feed and put the doll to bed.

Say

Let's put a blanket around this baby. Aiden, you are keeping that baby warm, just like a mommy or daddy would.

Jesus was a baby, too. We're glad that Jesus was born. Thank You, God, for Jesus.

Tip

One of the best ways to encourage a child to participate in an activity is to begin the activity yourself. For example, when a child is near you wrap a doll in a blanket and rock it. A child will often want to follow your example.

Quiet Play

Gift Bows

Collect

Colorful gift bows, at least two of each color
Bags

Do

Place bows into one or more bags. Give a bag to a toddler. As he or she takes a bow from the bag, talk about the child's actions and say the name of the color. Continue as long as child is interested.

Say

Terrell, you found a red bow. Can you find another red bow?

I'm glad to play with you. I love you and Jesus loves you. A long time ago, Jesus was a baby. I'm glad that Jesus was born.

I Love Jesus!

Do

Sit next to a toddler and hold up your hand as you say the following finger play. Point to a different finger as you name each person who loves Jesus.

> Who loves little baby Jesus?
> His mother, Mary, loved Him.
> Joseph loved Him.
> The shepherds loved Him.
> The wise men loved Him.
> And I love Him.

Gently hold the hand of the toddler and point to his or her fingers as you say the finger play again. Use the child's name in the last line.

Say

We love Jesus. Thank You, God, for sending Jesus. We're glad that Jesus was born!

Tip

Repeating the finger play several times to give a child time to anticipate what you will do.

Christmas Card Puzzles

Collect

Several Christmas cards with backs cut off
Clear Con-Tact paper
Scissors

Do

Cover cards with Con-Tact paper. Cut each card into two or three wide strips to make puzzles.

Give the puzzle pieces to a child and see if he or she can put the puzzle together. Be ready to give a clue to help child.

Say

Let's see if we can put this puzzle together. This piece goes on top. Which piece do you think comes next?

This puzzle shows a picture of an angel. Angels told people that Jesus was born. Jesus was a baby! We're glad Jesus was born.

Flashlight Fun

Collect

At least two flashlights

Do

Let children shine the flashlight in different areas of the room. (Optional: Darken the room enough to see the light.) Talk about the items on which children shine the light, connecting the items to Jesus' birth when possible.

Say

Brianna, you are shining the light on the doll bed. Jesus was a baby. Christmastime is Jesus' birthday!

We're glad Jesus was born.

January

God Helps Me to Grow

Jesus Grew
(See Luke 2:52.)

"God made us."
(See Malachi 2:10.)

· · · · · · · · · · · ·

This month you will help each child:

• associate new accomplishments with God and Jesus;

• enjoy the success of new accomplishments.

Devotional

Read Luke 2:21-40. Mary and Joseph must have closely observed their infant son in the days and weeks following their visit to the Temple. The prophecies of Anna and Simeon, added to the previous announcements by angels, undoubtedly stirred expectations of unusual qualities in their child. Would this child with such a special destiny show special abilities at an early age?

If Mary and Joseph had anticipated some dramatic evidence of Jesus' divine nature in the early years of His life, they must have been disappointed. After the excitement of the prophecies, life settled back into normal routines. Jesus gradually began to mature. The Gospels do not record any amazing intelligence, precocious abilities, or supernatural authority. Like all babies and toddlers, He simply continued to grow. Gradually, daily, He kept increasing "in wisdom and stature, and in favor with God and men" (Luke 2:52).

When we discover significant insights or have dramatic spiritual experiences, we often expect that life will suddenly become different. We are frequently disappointed that the impact of Sunday seems so weak on Monday. We would like to reach maturity in large, bold moves. We become impatient with the slow, small steps that seem to make so little difference.

Yet as Jesus grew normally through all the stages of infancy, childhood and adolescence, Scripture assures us the grace of God was upon Him (see Luke 2:40). That same grace works today in each Christian's heart and mind, guiding the gradual but powerful process of growth, as we seek to become more like Jesus.

During the month of January, display this poster at child's eye level. Talk about the baby and the girl in the poster and how God helps children grow.

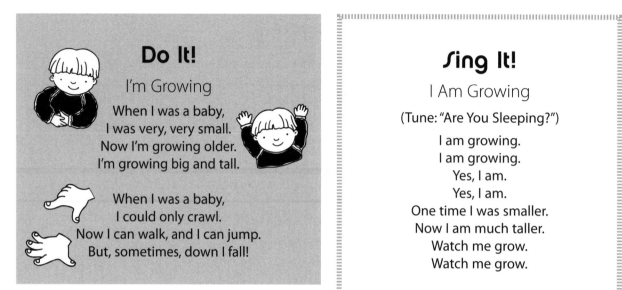

Do It!

I'm Growing

When I was a baby,
I was very, very small.
Now I'm growing older.
I'm growing big and tall.

When I was a baby,
I could only crawl.
Now I can walk, and I can jump.
But, sometimes, down I fall!

Sing It!

I Am Growing

(Tune: "Are You Sleeping?")

I am growing.
I am growing.
Yes, I am.
Yes, I am.
One time I was smaller.
Now I am much taller.
Watch me grow.
Watch me grow.

Tell It!

Jesus Grew

Once Jesus was a baby.
Jesus learned to crawl.
Then He learned to walk.
Jesus grew to be a bigger boy.
He learned to do many things.
You are growing, too.
You are learning to talk and sing and run
and climb.
God made you.
God will help you grow.
(See Luke 2:52.)

Display this poster at teacher's eye level in your nursery. Tell the Bible story, sing the song, do the finger play and repeat the Bible verse to one or more interested children.

Activities with Babies

Choose one or more of these learning activities to provide for babies during a session. Consider your facility, the number of babies and teachers and the supplies you have available as you plan which activities you will use. Continue the activity as long as the child is interested. For more information on using this curriculum, see "Why Use Curriculum?" on page 6.

God's Wonders

What Do You Feel?

Collect

Several of these touch-and-feel items: soft toy, small amount of water, towel, silk fabric, cotton ball, crumpled paper

Do

Gently stroke a baby's hand with a soft toy. Wet your hand and stroke the baby's hand, dripping a little water on it. Dab a towel on the baby's hands to dry up the water. Use other objects to stroke the baby.

Say

Tianna, God made your hands. Can you feel the cool water? The towel feels dry.

Thank You, God, for Tianna's hands. Thank You for making her hands to grow so big and strong.

Movement

Hold On

Do

While a baby is lying in the crib or sitting in your lap, offer a finger for him or her to grasp. Older babies may pull themselves to a sitting or standing position. Younger babies will simply enjoy pulling on your finger.

Say

Your hands are so strong! God made your strong hands!

God is helping you to grow.

Tip

Your smiles and conversation will encourage a baby who is learning to sit up, crawl or walk. Give assistance only when needed so the child can succeed.

Music

I'm Growing!

Collect

I Love to Sing! CD and player
Toy people or dolls

Do

While a baby is seated on the floor near you, play "Grow Song" and move the toy people or dolls rhythmically in time to the music. If a baby is interested, he or she may want to hold onto the items.

After the baby has lost interest in the toy people or dolls, continue to play and sing along with the song and gently tap the child's arms or legs in time to the music.

Say

Bailey, you are growing bigger every day! God is helping you to grow!

So Big!

Do

Talk with a baby about he or she is growing "so big." Raise your hands in the air when you say "so big." If the baby seems interested, gently raise the baby's hands when you say "so big."

Sing the words on the next page to the tune of "Are You Sleeping?" (also printed on the January Teaching Poster from *Nursery Posters*), raising the baby's arms when you sing "Now I am much taller."

I am growing.
I am growing.
Yes, I am.
Yes, I am.
One time I was smaller.
Now I am much taller.
Watch me grow.
Watch me grow.

Say

Lily, God is helping you to grow. You are growing bigger.

Pictures and Books

Growing All the Time

Collect

January Poster from *Nursery Posters* displayed at child's eye level

Sturdy books with pictures of people of different ages

Do

Show the poster or the book to a baby. Point to the people and talk about how they have grown.

Say

I see a baby and a big sister in this picture.

Calvin, you're a baby now, but you are growing. God helps you to grow.

Jesus Grew Like You

Collect

Bible Story Picture from *I Love to Look!* or *Nursery Posters*

Do

Show and talk about the picture.

Let a baby hold the picture if desired. Connect the child's action with the story.

Say

Devin, this is a picture of Jesus. Jesus grew

and learned to sit up and crawl and walk. You are growing, too.

God helps you to grow.

Quiet Play

Make a Noise

Do

Make any of the following sounds while you are near a baby or holding him or her: "coo coo," kissing sound, tongue clicking, "ch, ch" sound, blowing air out or in.

Repeat a sound several times. If the baby responds by making the sound, then repeat the sound enthusiastically back to the baby.

Say

I like to hear you make new sounds, Brittany. God made your mouth. God made your tongue.

God helps you grow and make new sounds.

Tip

This activity can also be done when you are rocking a baby or changing his or her diaper. Focus your attention on the baby and take advantage of this one-on-one time.

What Do You See?

Collect

Variety of toys

Wall-mounted mirror or large child-safe mirror

Do

While a baby is lying on his or her stomach, place one or two toys in front of the baby to look at. Describe the things the baby sees.

Then position the baby in front of a wall-mounted mirror or prop up a mirror in front of the baby. Point to the baby's eyes, nose, mouth and ears in the mirror and talk about them.

Say

There's Samantha! God made your eyes to see so many things. Thank You, God, for Samantha's eyes.

Look in the mirror and you can see you are growing so big! God helps you to grow.

Activities with Toddlers

Choose one or more of the learning activities on pages 45-48 to provide for toddlers during a session. Consider your facility, the number of children and teachers and the supplies you have available as you plan which activities you will use. The best kind of teaching for toddlers will happen as you take advantage of teachable moments as children play and experience the learning activities you have provided. Continue an activity as long as one or more children are interested. For more information on using this curriculum, see "Why Use Curriculum?" on page 6.

Active Play

Where's the Toy?

Collect

Two identical toys

Do

Show the child two identical toys. Put one toy somewhere in the room. Put the other toy in front of the child.

Say, "Here is a red block. Can you find the other red block?"

If the child doesn't see the other block, bring the child with you to get the block. Play game several times.

Say

We found the red block! God made your eyes so you can see the red blocks.

God made you!

Play Ball

Collect

One or more clean, child-safe balls (beach balls, basketballs, soccer balls or volleyballs)

Do

Sit or stand next to a child. Push a ball away from you. After you or the child retrieves the ball, push the ball away again. Give the child time to bring the ball back.

Say

Delaney, you have such strong arms and legs. You can go and get the ball and push or carry it back all by yourself.

God helps you grow and try new things.

Shape Walking

Collect

Large circles, triangles and squares approximately 12 inches (30 cm) in size cut from different colors of construction paper

Masking tape

Do

Use tape to attach the shapes to the floor in a path. Encourage children to walk on the shapes. Say each shape's name and color.

Say

I am stepping on a red circle. Now it's your turn! Kenna, you walk so well. God made your legs to grow and move. Thank You, God, for helping Kenna to grow and walk.

Tip

A toddler's attention span is very short so he or she will change activities quickly. Look for an opportunity to repeat the activity later with the child.

Growing Up Tall

Collect

Several scarves

Do

Give a child a scarf and hold one scarf yourself.

Crouch low. Then stand up high and wave the scarf. Encourage the child to imitate you.

Say

Let's see how little you can be. Now let's see how tall you can be.

You are growing taller.

God helps you grow every day.

Art Play

Handprints

Collect

Sheet of paper for each child
Crayon

Do

While a toddler is nearby, trace around one of your hands on a sheet of paper. If a child is interested, trace around his or her hands, too.

Say

Garrett, I traced your hand. Do you want me to trace your other hand, too? You are growing. Your hands are getting bigger!

God helps you to grow.

Music

Movin' Music

Collect

I Love to Sing! Music CD (or other lively children's music) and player

Do

Play "Grow Song" (or other music) and lead children in a variety of actions: clapping, waving, patting head, etc.

Say

Look at all the things you have learned to do. Gabriella, you are growing bigger just like God plans for you to grow.

God helps you grow. God planned for your arms and legs to grow strong.

Tip: Personalizing the words of this song by using the child's name in the song will increase the child's interest in the activity.

God's Wonders

Rainbow Colors

Collect

Large, sturdy resealable bags
Water
Food coloring in several colors

Do

Before class, fill several bags half full with water. Add several drops of food coloring to each bag, making a different color in each bag. Place each bag in another bag and seal.

In class, children look at and handle bags, gently patting them. Talk about the colors they see.

Say

Thomas, you are holding the bag with blue water in it. God made your eyes so you can see colors. God made you! God is helping you to grow.

Delaney, pat the bag with your hand. God made your hands so you can do lots of things. I'm glad you are growing bigger.

Look at My Doll

Collect

Doll

Do

Use a doll to demonstrate the different parts of a child's body; then ask the toddler to find his or her own eye, arm, leg, feet, etc.

Talk about the fact that God made us.

Say

Bella, here are this doll's feet. Where are your feet? God made your feet.

God made you. God helps you grow bigger every day. Thank You, God.

Pictures and Books

Growing Every Day

Collect

Bible Story Picture from *I Love to Look!* or *Nursery Posters*

Sturdy books picturing children at different stages of growth: a baby sleeping, then crawling, and walking

Do

Show and talk about the pictures. Describe how God helps children to grow and do new things.

Say

Jesus grew and learned to crawl and then walk just like you!

We can thank God for helping you to grow and do new things! Thank You, God!

Tip: Display posters at child's eye level. If possible, display the poster near an area where children play with toys. Then look for ways to connect the child's activity with the way in which Jesus grew as a young child.

Pretend Play

All Aboard

Collect

Two toddler-sized chairs

Do

Place chairs together to form a pretend car. Invite a child to sit on a chair. Ask the child to drive you to the store, to church or to the park.

Talk about what you "see" along the drive and at each place.

Say

Annissa, you can be the driver of the car. We are driving to so many places. You're growing bigger, Annissa, so you can go lots of different places!

God made you. God helps you to grow!

Growing Talk

Collect

Toy telephone

Do

With the telephone, sit down by a toddler. Make the sound of a ringing phone, and then pick up the receiver. Talk on the phone to the child, describing what the child is doing.

Invite the child to talk on the phone, too. Each time you talk on the phone, comment about a different part of the child's body that is growing (legs, arms, feet, etc.).

Say

Hi, Kayley. How are you today? I see you're using your hands to play with the farm animals. Your hands are getting bigger! God made you! God helps you to grow!

God loves you.

What's for Dinner?

Collect

Toy dishes, cups
Napkins

Do

Children take turns placing dishes, cups and napkins on a table. Children pretend to serve food and drinks.

God gives you good food to help you grow. God loves you, Shandra.

When we eat good food, our bodies grow. I'm glad God helps us grow.

Quiet Play

What's that Sound?

Collect

Several toys or objects that make sounds (bells, rattles, shakers, etc.)

Cloth or paper bag

Do

Place one toy or object inside the bag. Shake the bag for a child to hear.

Let the child take a turn to shake the bag and/or pull the toy or object out of the bag. Repeat with other toys and objects.

Say

I hear the bell. Cameron, can you hear the bell?

God made your ears to hear. God helps you to grow and hear sounds.

Puppet Friends

Collect

One or more hand animal puppets

Do

Put a puppet on your hand. Softly talk to the child about what he or she is wearing, and the ways in which the child is growing. If the child is interested, put the puppet on the child's hand.

Say

Hi, Jolie. I'm glad to see you today. You are wearing a blue dress with white flowers on it. I see your strong legs. God made your legs. God is helping your legs grow bigger and stronger.

God planned for your legs to grow strong so you can have fun walking and running. Thank You, God, for our legs.

Beanbag Fun

Collect

Several child-safe beanbags

Do

Let children hold and play with beanbags. Children may carry them around the room, put them into containers, drop them, put them on their heads, etc.

Say

We're having fun playing with these beanbags. Damon, you put the beanbag on your head. You are learning to do so many new things!

You are growing bigger, just like God plans for you to grow. God loves you!

Bead in a Cup

Collect

One or two large wooden beads (too large to swallow)

At least two plastic cups

Do

Show the child how to pour the bead from one cup to the other. Let an interested child have a turn to pour the bead back and forth.

Say

Niki, I see that you can pour the bead from the red cup to the blue cup. You are learning to do new things every day. God is helping you to grow.

God made you and He helps you grow.

Tip

Keep a camera handy. As you see a child having a particularly good time, take a picture. After printing the picture, talk about it with the child and then send it home to parents.

February

My Family Loves Me

Timothy Learned About God's Love
(See 2 Timothy 1:5; 3:15.)

"God gives us families."
(See Psalm 68:6.)

This month you will help each child:

• begin to associate God and Jesus with loving people at home and at church;

• respond to demonstrations of affection.

Devotional

Three short verses about Timothy's early years tantalize us. Read Acts 16:1; 2 Timothy 1:5; 3:15. There is so much more we would like to know. How did his mother and grandmother go about teaching him the Scriptures? At what age did they begin their instruction? In what ways did Lois and Eunice share their faith with Timothy? How did they overcome the difficulty of Timothy's father probably being an unbeliever?

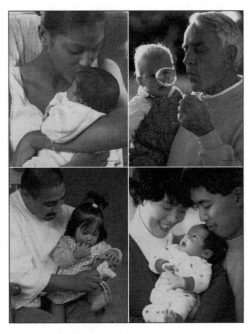

All we see are the results. Perhaps it is best that Paul did not share Eunice's child-raising "secrets." Every parent since would have felt compelled to follow the same exact procedures, possibly losing sight of the one crucial fact that the apostle Paul shares in this letter to Timothy, now an adult. Paul tells us that both Lois and Eunice possessed a sincere faith. Their task was to help make this faith meaningful to young Timothy. Because Christ dwelt within them, it was natural for His love to flow through them to Timothy. There must have been times of struggle and disappointment for Lois and Eunice, but sincere faith in Christ gave them a steady foundation.

As you seek to minister to young children, first make sure that Jesus is your Savior and Lord. Then your ministry to little ones will be based in the sincerity of personal experience.

During the month of February, display this poster at child's eye level. Talk about the way in which family members are showing love to their children.

Do It!

Families

We all live in families,
You and me.
What kinds of families?
Let me see!
Tall ones and short ones;
Big ones and small ones.
We all live in families,
You and me.

♪ing It!

My Family

(Tune: "Row, Row, Row Your Boat")

Thank, thank, thank You, God
For my family!
God made families to love
And care for you and me!

Tell It!

Timothy Learned About God's Love

Timothy was a little child, just like you.
Timothy liked good things to eat,
And he liked to play, just like you.
Timothy's mommy and
grandma loved God.
They taught him about God.
Timothy learned that God
loves boys and girls
And grown-ups, too.
Timothy learned to love God,
just like you.
(See 2 Timothy 1:5; 3:15.)

Display this poster at teacher's eye level in your nursery. Tell the Bible story, sing the song, do the finger play and repeat the Bible verse to one or more interested children.

Activities with Babies

Choose one or more of these learning activities to provide for babies during a session. Consider your facility, the number of babies and teachers and the supplies you have available as you plan which activities you will use. Continue the activity as long as the child is interested. For more information on using this curriculum, see "Why Use Curriculum?" on page 6.

God's Wonders

Touch of Water

Collect
Lukewarm water
Plastic bowl
Soft towel

Do
Put a small amount of lukewarm water in a plastic bowl. Hold a baby so he or she can touch the water. (Or hold a baby near a sink to feel running water from a faucet.)
Have towel ready to dry the baby's hands.

Say
Your mommy and daddy use water to give you a bath. God made mommies and daddies to take care of their children.
I'm glad God gives us families.

Movement

Crawling Fun

Collect
Firm pillow
Toy

Do
On one side of a firm pillow, set a baby who can crawl. Sit on the floor on the other side of the object, holding a toy in your hand.
Invite the baby to crawl toward you around or across the pillow.

Say
I'm so glad I get to play with you, Leticia. Your big sister likes to play with you, too. God gives us families.
Thank You, God, for Leticia. Thank You, God, for Leticia's family.

Music

Hold Me!

Collect
I Love to Sing! CD and player

Do
Hold a baby so that his or her head is at your shoulder. As you walk around the room or rock the baby, play "My Family Cares."
Continue singing or humming. Young children enjoy the combination of singing and movement.

Say
I'm glad to hold you, Sophia. Your mom and dad love to hold you, too. God gave you a family to take good care of you.
We can thank God for your family.

Tip
This activity may help to soothe a baby who is tired or who could use some special attention.

My Happy Family

Collect
I Love to Sing! CD and player
Picture of each child and at least one family member

Do
Show child the picture of his or her family

while you play "Happy Family." Point to the picture of the child's mom or dad and the child as you sing the appropriate words.

Say

Juan, I'm so glad you and your family came to church today. God gave you a family.

Your family loves you!

Pictures and Books

Family Time Books

Collect

February Poster from *Nursery Posters* displayed at child's eye level

One or more sturdy books with pictures of families

Do

Look at pictures of families with a baby. Talk about the pictures with the children.

Say

Look at this mom. She is holding her baby. And here is a grandpa playing with a baby. Moms and dads, grandmas and grandpas love their children.

I'm glad God gives us families. Your mom and dad love you!

Tip

When children show interest in your conversation, repeat it several times.

Who's in My Family?

Collect

Bible Story Picture from *I Love to Look!* or *Nursery Posters*

Do

Show and talk about the Bible Story Picture, naming and pointing to the people. Tell the brief story.

Say

Here is a picture of Timothy. Can you see his mom? Here is his grandma. Timothy's family loved him. They told him about Jesus.

Jackson, your family loves you. God gives us families.

Quiet Play

Where's Little Mouse?

Do

Starting at the baby's feet, walk your fingers up the child's body, saying, "Little mouse, little mouse, where will you go?"

As your fingers walk up to the baby's neck, say in a squeaky mouse voice, "Up to your chin to tickle you so!" Then gently tickle the baby's neck under his or her chin. Do this several times if the child is enjoying the game.

Say

It's fun to play with you, Madeline. Your dad likes to play with you, too! God gave you a dad. Your dad loves you and plays with you.

Wiggle Worm

Collect

Washable stuffed animal

Do

Sit on the floor with a baby. Hold a stuffed animal in your hand. Move the animal slightly while saying a silly sentence in a funny voice: "Hi there, Wiggle Worm."

Repeat the sentence using a variety of voices (soft, high, low, etc.) and holding the stuffed animal in a different place each time (near, away from, behind and to the side of the baby).

Say

Isabella, I'm glad your mom and dad brought you to church today. Your mom and dad love you!

God gives us families who love us. Thank You, God, for our families.

My Family Loves Me

Activities with Toddlers

Choose one or more of the learning activities on pages 53-56 to provide for toddlers during a session. Consider your facility, the number of children and teachers and the supplies you have available as you plan which activities you will use. The best kind of teaching for toddlers will happen as you take advantage of teachable moments as children play and experience the learning activities you have provided. Continue an activity as long as one or more children are interested. For more information on using this curriculum, see "Why Use Curriculum?" on page 6.

Active Play

Throwing Fun

Collect

Empty container (basket, large paper bag)
Soft ball

Do

Throw or drop the ball into the container.
Let a child throw or drop the ball into the container. Repeat several times.

Say

Lydia, we're having fun playing ball. Who plays ball with you at home? Your dad and your mom play with you. Your family loves you.

Tip

Before children arrive, place several favorite toys on the floor. The first children need only a few toy options as they begin play. Add two or more new toys periodically as more children arrive.

Families on the Go

Collect

Masking tape
Toy cars and people

Do

On the floor, use masking tape to mark off a road with at least one intersection. (Remove tape after activity.)
Child uses toy cars and people to drive on the road.

Say

Look at the families driving on this road. I see a mommy driving a car. Where do you think she's going, Lucas?
Mommies love their children. God gives us mommies to take care of us.

Riding in My Car

Collect

Several ride-on cars or other vehicles

Do

Invite children to ride cars or other vehicles around the room.

Say

Gabrielle, you are driving the car. Your family goes to lots of places together.
God gives us families. Our families love us. Thank You, God, for our families.

Build a House

Collect

Large cardboard blocks
Toy people (too large to choke on) representing a variety of family members

Do

Build a house with the blocks. Pretend that toy people are family members. Give an interested child one or more toy people to play with.

Say

Angelina, God gave you a dad to take you for walks and play with you. I'm glad God gives us families. Our families love us.

Art Play

Paper Plate Family

Collect

Paper plates
Jumbo crayons

Do

Draw faces on the
paper plates. Let children color the plates.

Hold one plate in front of your face and pretend to be a mom or dad and talk about ways that person shows love to family members.

Let an interested child hold a paper plate, too.

Say

I'm the mommy in this family. I love my little child. Are you the daddy? Daddies love their children.

God made daddies and mommies to love their children. Thank You, God, for daddies and mommies.

Valentines

Collect

Red construction paper
Scissors
Valentine stickers
Jumbo crayons

Do

Before class, cut heart shapes out of construction paper.

In class, invite one or two children at a time to make a valentine. Children decorate valentines with stickers and crayons.

Say

Elijah, you can make a valentine to give to your mom. Your mom takes good care of you.

Mommies and daddies love their children. God gives us families to take care of us.

God's Wonders

Wash and Dry

Collect

Plastic dishpan (or baby tub) with a small amount of water in it
Washable doll
Several towels

Do

Set dishpan on a towel. Let children wash a doll in the water, and then dry it with a towel. Repeat as long as children are interested.

Say

Do you like to take a bath? Let's give this doll a bath. Your grandma gives you a bath and takes care of you. God made your grandma to care for you.

God gives us families. Our families love us.

Colored Viewers

Collect

Several transparent plastic (acetate) report covers in bright colors

Do

Children look through the plastic sheets. Describe the people and objects the child is looking at.

Look through a plastic sheet yourself and describe what you see.

Say

Fernando, you are looking through the blue paper. Who do you see?

I like to play with you. Your grandpa likes to play with you, too. Our families love us!

I'm glad God gives us families.

Music

Follow the Leader

Collect

I Love to Sing! CD and player

Do

Play "Happy Family." When a child is near you, begin to clap your hands in time to the music. Invite a child to clap hands, too. When a child imitates you, smile and acknowledge the child's actions.

As the music continues to play, use a variety of motions: wave or shake your hands, stamp your foot, pat your shoulder, touch your toes, or rock from side to side.

Say

Eden, you are clapping your hands! It's fun to clap our hands!

This song talks about our families. We love our families. We're glad God gives us families.

Telephone Songs

Collect

I Love to Sing! CD and player
One or two toy telephones

Do

Play "My Family Cares" while you sit near a child on the floor. Pretend to talk on a telephone and sing along with the song. A child may want to imitate your action and use a telephone, too.

Say

Morgan, do you want to sing on the telephone? I'm singing about all the things we can do with our families.

God loves us and made our families to care for us. Thank You, God, for the people in Morgan's family.

Pictures and Books

Family Photos

Collect

Photo of each child's family; optional—take instant or digital photo of child and family member when child arrives
Resealable bags
Stapler

Do

Put each photo in a separate resealable bag. Staple bags together to form a book.

Look at the photos with a child.

Say

Look at this picture of your family. Can you point to your mommy? Where is your daddy? Where are you?

Isaac, your family loves you! God planned for you to have a mom and a dad and three brothers. God loves you!

A Bible-Times Family

Collect

February Bible Story Picture from *I Love to Look!* or *Nursery Posters*

Do

Show and talk about the family in the Bible Story Picture. Relate the people in the picture to the child and his or her family.

Say

Alexa, here's a picture of a boy named Timothy. The Bible tells us that Timothy learned about Jesus. Here is Timothy's mom and grandma. Timothy's family loved him.

God gives us families who love us.

Tip

Take the Bible Story Picture card to an area of the room where children are playing. Show a child the picture to attract interest. If the child is not interested right then, it's OK. Try again later.

Pretend Play

My House

Collect
Two chairs
Blanket or bed sheet

Do
Drape the blanket or bed sheet over the two chairs to form a "house," leaving one side of the house completely open. (Optional: Set up a play tent.)

A toddler will enjoy going in and out of the playhouse, as well as transporting objects into and out of the house.

Say
Here is our house. Who is in our house today? I see Keira. Keira is pretending to be her mom. God gives us moms to love us and take care of us. Your mom loves you, Keira.

Play Family

Collect
Toy people representing family members
Blocks and/or one or more small boxes

Do
Turn the small box on its side, or build a simple house outline with blocks.

Hand the child each toy person as you name it. Pretend to have the family members feed and play with the children.

Say
Carson, here's the mommy in this family. Here's the brother and here's the baby. The mommy takes care of and plays with the baby.

God loves you, Carson. God gave you a mommy and a brother to love you! Thank You, God, for Carson's family.

Who Helps Me?

Collect
One or more child-sized cleaning items (vacuum, broom, mop, etc.)

Do
Let children pretend to use the cleaning items. Talk about the ways families help each other.

Say
Daniel, you are doing a good job vacuuming our room. Who uses the vacuum at home? God planned for people in families to help each other.

Your mom and dad help you when you are at your house. You can help your family, too. God gives us families!

Quiet Play

Family Fingers

Do
Gently wiggle one of the child's fingers as you say each line of the following rhyme. Adapt the names of family members to fit the child's family.

As you say the last line, run your finger over all the fingers on the child's hand.

This is the daddy, he's smiling at you.
This is the mommy, she's happy, too.
This is the brother, he plays with you.
This is the sister, she loves you, too.
And here is Jonah, he's glad to see
All of these people in his family.

Say
It's fun to talk about our families. I'm glad God gives us families. Thank You, God!

Tip
If you have trouble remembering the words of this rhyme, use the finger fun on the February Teaching Poster (mounted on wall in your nursery).

March

Jesus Loves Me

Jesus Loved Zacchaeus
(See Luke 19:1-6.)

"Jesus loves us."
(See Revelation 1:5.)

This month you will help each child:

• enjoy activities in which teachers talk lovingly of Jesus;

• frequently hear the words "Jesus loves us."

Devotional

Zacchaeus was a hated man. He boldly enriched himself at the expense of others, hiding behind the authority of the Roman government, hurting people right and left. His behavior was a lot like what we might see in a cranky toddler—grabby, aggressive, unable to focus on anyone but himself.

While Zacchaeus's focus on "ME" and "MINE!" was a normal response when he (himself) was only a baby or toddler, he seems to have never grown beyond it to treat other people with compassion. Instead, he became an adult who was just plain selfish and cruel. Do you suppose he was treated cruelly as a little one, teaching him that cruelty was acceptable when one got big enough or powerful enough to bully other people? Did he live with selfishness that taught him it was the way to live? Although it's true that children learn what they live with, it may have been none of those factors. But whatever the cause may have been, the only cure for his childish attitude was Jesus' love!

You may feel like there's a child or two in your nursery with real "Zacchaeus potential"! But remember that it is Jesus' love that changes people—no matter what their age or height or problem. And Jesus' love can flow through you as you sing, play, feed and change these little ones who learn what they live. Take time before you enter the nursery to ask Him to give you His love to share. He loves to answer such prayers! And recognize that as you treat these little ones with love—the kind of love God has shown you in Jesus—you are teaching powerful lessons, lessons that may help your babies outgrow the "Zacchaeus Syndrome"!

During the month of March, display this poster at child's eye level. Talk about Jesus' love for children and the way in which the dad in the poster is showing love and care for his child.

Do It!
Day and Night

When the sun is in the sky,
Jesus loves me.
When the stars are way up high,
Jesus loves me.
In the day and in the night,
While I play and then sleep tight,
Jesus loves me.

Sing It!
Yes, Jesus Loves You

(Tune: Refrain to "Jesus Loves Me")

Yes, Jesus loves you.
Yes, Jesus loves you.
Yes, Jesus loves you!
The Bible tells us so.

Tell It!
Jesus Loved Zacchaeus

Zacchaeus wanted to see Jesus.
But Zacchaeus was little.
Zacchaeus couldn't see
over the taller people.
So he climbed up into a tree!
Now he could see Jesus.
Jesus saw Zacchaeus, too.
Jesus loved Zacchaeus.
And Jesus loves you!
(See Luke 19:1-6.)

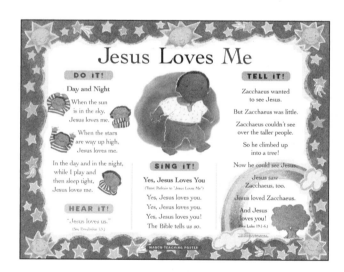

Display this poster at teacher's eye level in your nursery. Tell the Bible story, sing the song, do the finger play and repeat the Bible verse to one or more interested children.

Activities with Babies

Choose one or more of these learning activities to provide for babies during a session. Consider your facility, the number of babies and teachers and the supplies you have available as you plan which activities you will use. Continue the activity as long as the child is interested. For more information on using this curriculum, see "Why Use Curriculum?" on page 6.

God's Wonders

Soft and Furry

Collect

Several washable stuffed animals

Do

One at a time, hold a stuffed animal near a baby so he or she can touch it, pat it and hold it.

Say

Katherine, this little bunny feels soft. You can hold the bunny.

I'm glad you are here today. Jesus loves you, Katherine. I'm glad Jesus loves us.

Tip

Babies will explore the stuffed animals using hands and mouths. Remove an animal that has been in a child's mouth.

Movement

Scarf Play

Collect

Several colorful scarves (bandannas or pieces of lightweight fabric may also be used)

Do

Give a baby a scarf. Hold a scarf yourself. Wave your scarf, smiling and nodding your head as the baby watches you. The baby may imitate your actions.

Also use the scarf to play a gentle tugging game with a baby.

Say

You're playing with the scarf, Claire. Jesus loves you when you play. Jesus loves you all the time!

Thank You, Jesus, for loving us.

Music

Swing and Sing

Collect

I Love to Sing! CD and player

Do

Play "Jesus Loves Me" while holding a baby in your arms. Rock the baby in a swinging motion while the music plays. Hold an older baby with your hands around his or her waist. Bend over and gently swing the child between your legs in time to the music. After several swings, stop and hold the baby in your arms.

A baby who has enjoyed the swinging motion will often indicate pleasure by wiggling or making happy sounds. Repeat the swinging activity several more times.

Say

We're glad that Jesus loves us. And I'm glad that you are here today!

Cole, Jesus loves you. Jesus loves all our friends here today.

Jesus Loves You

Collect

I Love to Sing! CD and player
Picture of Jesus

Do

Show a baby a picture of Jesus. Play and sing along with "Thank You, Jesus," replacing the word "me" in the song with the child's name.

Then sound out the rhythm of the song by tapping your toe, clapping your hands, or by making clicking noises with your tongue.

Say

I'm so glad that I can sing with you, Kayla. I like to be with you. Jesus loves you and so do I.

Pictures and Books

Jesus and the Children

Collect

Sturdy book that pictures Jesus and children

Do

Show the book to a baby while holding him or her on your lap. Point to Jesus and say His name. Describe the children pictured in the book.

Say

Here is a picture of Jesus. Jesus loves children. I see a little girl and a little boy in this book. Jesus loves girls. Jesus loves boys. Julia, Jesus loves you!

The Bible Tells Me So

Collect

Sturdy children's Bible

Do

Show the Bible to a child and talk about Jesus' love for the child. Turn the pages of the Bible for the child to see the pictures and words.

Say

This book is called a Bible. The Bible tells us that Jesus loves us. Jesus loves you. (Optional: Sing the words of "Jesus Loves Me" while looking at the Bible together.)

Thank You, Jesus, for loving us.

Tip

Use the child's name frequently during your conversation.

Quiet Play

Slowly, Slowly

Collect

Soft blanket, washable stuffed animal, baby toy

Do

Gently and slowly move your finger from a baby's shoulder down to his or her hand. Describe your actions. Repeat the action several times. Then use another object (blanket, stuffed animal or toy) to touch the baby.

If the baby seems interested in what you are doing, repeat the activity, this time moving your fingers quickly and using the word "quickly" to describe your actions.

Say

I am going to slowly, slowly touch you on your arm. Can you feel my finger? I like to play with you.

Jesus loves you and I do, too.

What's Out There?

Collect

Toy that makes a sound, moves or lights up when touched

Do

Set a baby on a blanket on the floor. Place a toy where the child can see it, but cannot reach it without moving slightly. While the baby is watching you, move the toy. Wait to see if the baby tries to grasp the toy. If the baby is interested, but can't reach it yet, move it close enough for the baby to reach.

Say

James, I can see that you like this light-up toy. I love to play with you.

Jesus loves you, James. I love you, too!

Activities with Toddlers

Choose one or more of the learning activities on pages 61-64 to provide for toddlers during a session. Consider your facility, the number of children and teachers and the supplies you have available as you plan which activities you will use. The best kind of teaching for toddlers will happen as you take advantage of teachable moments as children play and experience the learning activities you have provided. Continue an activity as long as one or more children are interested. For more information on using this curriculum, see "Why Use Curriculum?" on page 6.

Active Play

Climb and Stretch

Collect

Climbing structure (bridge, climbing toy, etc.)
Picture of a tree (covered with clear Con-Tact paper for durability)

Do

Encourage a child to climb on the structure. You may also hold the picture high enough so a child has to stretch his or her arms to touch it.

Say

Henry, you're climbing up the steps. The Bible tells about a man named Zacchaeus. Zacchaeus climbed up a tree. He wanted to see Jesus. Jesus loved Zacchaeus.

Jesus loves us, too!

Pop Up!

Do

Stand near a child. While the child is watching you, bend down to the floor. Then as you say "Pop!" pop up quickly, reaching your arms up and out and spreading your fingers. Do this several times and invite the child to "play pop up" with you, too.

Say

Let's play Pop Up together. Watch what I do. Then you can have a turn.

You're playing, Mackenzie! Jesus loves you while you play. Jesus loves you all the time!

Tip

Children will experience Jesus' love at church when they are having enjoyable experiences with loving teachers who talk and sing about Jesus.

Seesaw

Do

Sit on the floor facing a toddler. Hold out your hands and invite the child to play seesaw with you.

Lean back and forth, gently pulling on the child's hands and saying the words "back and forth."

Say

Nicole, let's hold hands and play seesaw. I'm glad you came today so that we can play. Jesus loves you, Nicole.

At church, we learn that Jesus loves us. Thank You, Jesus, for Your love.

Bridges

Collect

Blocks
Toy people
Small balls (too large to swallow)

Do

Use blocks to build at least one bridge. Invite a child to move toy people under the bridges.

Children may also roll small balls under the bridges.

Say

Look at all the children walking under this bridge! Jesus loves children. Jesus loves you, Jayden.

Julian, let's roll these balls under the bridge. I'm glad you're having fun at church today. Jesus loves you.

Art Play

Who Does Jesus Love?

Collect

Sheet of paper for each child
Marker
Jumbo crayons

Do

While a child is watching, print his or her name on a sheet of paper while you ask, "Who does Jesus love?" Say the child's name and point to it.

If a child is interested, he or she may color on the paper.

Say

There's your name, Wyatt! Jesus loves you. We're glad that Jesus loves us!

Color the Tree

Collect

Bible Story Picture from *I Love to Look!* or *Nursery Posters*
Large sheet of paper
Brown and green jumbo crayons
Tape

Do

On the paper, draw a simple outline of a large tree (see sketch).

Show and talk about the Bible Story Picture. Let children color the tree using brown and green crayons. Tape the tree onto a wall at child's eye level.

Say

The Bible tells us about a man who climbed a tree. His name was Zacchaeus. Zacchaeus wanted to see Jesus. Jesus loved him. We can color this tree with our green and brown crayons.

Sam, I see that you are coloring with the green crayon. Jesus loves you, too.

God's Wonders

Measure Me!

Collect

Length of butcher paper
Tape
Measuring stick
Crayon

Do

Tape paper to wall in an area where children can stand.

Ask a child to stand with his or her back against the paper. Make a mark on the paper to show how tall the child is. Write child's name near the mark.

Say

Gerardo, let's see how tall you are. I'm glad you came to church today. Jesus loves you.

The Bible tells us that Jesus loves us! Thank You, Jesus, for Your love.

Leaf Display

Collect

Bible Story Picture from *I Love to Look!* or *Nursery Posters*
Several real or artificial leaves of varying sizes and shapes
Sturdy paper plate or tray

Do

Show and talk about the Bible Story Picture.
Place leaves on plate or tray. Let children look at and handle the leaves.

Say

The Bible tells us about a man named Zacchaeus. He climbed a tree so he could see Jesus. Jesus loved Zacchaeus. Jesus loves us, too.

Let's look at these leaves. Here is a long narrow leaf. Here is a wide leaf.

Tip

If using real leaves, use only with teacher supervision. Store items out of children's reach.

Music

Jump and Clap!

Collect

I Love to Sing! CD and player

Do

Play "Jesus Loves Us All," jumping and clapping according to the song. Talk about Jesus' love.

Say

Let's sing a song about Jesus' love. We'll jump and clap in our song! Sean, can you jump with me? Can you clap?

We're happy to know that Jesus loves us!

Tip

Toddlers are likely to bend and then straighten their knees when you ask them to jump. That's OK; they will enjoy the music and the effort of trying to jump.

"Jesus Loves Me" Motions

Collect

March Teaching Poster from *Nursery Posters*

Do

Sing "Jesus Loves Me" to a child (see words on poster and on p. 58), replacing the word "me" with the child's name.

Use simple motions for words of this song. If the song and motions are repeated often enough, the child may soon join in on one or more motions.

Say

Jesus loves all the children. Jesus loves Brooke. Jesus loves Blake. Jesus loves Juliana and Owen.

Every day, no matter where we are, we can remember that Jesus loves us.

Pictures and Books

Where's Jesus?

Collect

Sturdy book with pictures of Jesus

Do

Bring a book with pictures of Jesus and sit near a child. Before opening the book, say, "Where's the picture of Jesus? Let's see if we can find a picture of Jesus."

As you or the child turn the pages, point to each picture of Jesus. Say, "There is Jesus! We found His picture!"

Say

Look, Taylor, there is Jesus! Jesus loves you. Jesus loves children.

At church we learn that Jesus loves us.

My Jesus Book

Collect

Several sheets of construction paper

Several pictures of Jesus (available from discarded Sunday School papers, church picture file, etc.)

Clear Con-Tact paper pieces cut slightly larger than the pictures

Do

Fold each sheet of paper in half to make a book. Place picture of Jesus inside the book and attach by covering picture with Con-Tact paper. Repeat, making several books (or one for each child, if possible).

Let a child look at a book. Talk about Jesus' love.

Say

Here is a book. Maria, can you open the book? Look! You found a picture of Jesus. Jesus loves you, Maria.

Thank You, Jesus, for loving Maria.

Pretend Play

Night and Day

Collect

Two or more dolls

Two or more blankets

Do

Give a child a doll to hold. Hold a doll yourself. Pretend to put your doll to sleep by wrapping the doll with a blanket.

Then pretend to wake up the doll. Talk about the things the doll is going to eat and drink.

Say

Carson, it's time to put our dolls to bed. They are sleepy. We go to bed when we're sleepy, too. Jesus loves you when you sleep.

Jesus loves you all the time.

Pack Up a Bag

Collect

Large paper bag (with handles, if possible)

Variety of small toys

Do

Set the paper bag on the floor. Invite a child to pack up the bag with several toys from the room. Describe the toys as child puts them in the bag. Ask a child to tell where he or she would like to go with the toys.

When the child tires of putting toys in the bag, he or she will have just as much fun taking out the items.

Say

Ian, I see you've put a blue car in the bag. And now you're putting the blocks in the bag.

Where should we take our bag? Should we take it to the part so we can play? Jesus loves us when we're at the park. Jesus loves us wherever we go.

Everywhere I Go

Collect

Toys that represent one or two different locations (house, farm, etc.)

Toy people (too large to swallow) and toy cars

Do

Arrange location toys several feet from each other. Children move the people from place to place.

Say

Let's pretend we're going to the farm. Let's move our people to the farm. Jesus loves us when we're at a farm. Jesus loves us everywhere we go.

Jonah, you put the little boy in the car. Jesus loves you when you are riding in the car. Jesus loves you everywhere you go.

Thank You, Jesus, for loving us.

Quiet Play

I See Someone Jesus Loves

Do

While sitting near a child, describe the child and then say the child's name. Repeat, until each child in the group has been described.

Say

I see someone Jesus loves. It's a girl wearing a red shirt. Who is it? That's right! Jesus loves Jordan.

Let's find out who else Jesus loves. I see someone with giraffes on his shirt. Who is it? That's right! Jesus loves Darnel.

I'm glad Jesus loves us.

Tip

Children love to hear their names over and over again. Use names frequently in your conversation, and play simple name games such as I See Someone Jesus Loves.

64 ●

April

God Makes Growing Things

God Made the World
(See Genesis 1:11-31.)

"God made everything."
(See Genesis 1:1.)

• • • • • • • • • • •

This month you will help each child:

• associate God with items of His creation;

• enjoy exploring items that God has made.

Devotional

And . . . it was good. These familiar words echo through the first chapter of Genesis. In springtime they seem to take on fresh luster as plants awaken from their long winter dormancy. There is something very good about new beginnings. Read Genesis 1:1-31.

Perhaps your spiritual life needs a new beginning, a reawakening from a period of seeming barrenness. Just as God's Spirit moved to bring beauty and order in the world's beginning, God Himself can bring light and life to the soul of anyone who is open to this love. God designed people in His own image to possess qualities that respond to His presence.

The good beginning for all creation came as God spoke. His Word still speaks today. Make time in your daily routines to read the Scriptures, asking God to help you respond.

Keep in mind that even the universe was not built in a day; six were needed to do the job! Expect God's work in your life to take place over a period of time as you gain spiritual insight according to His plan for you.

During the month of April, display this poster at child's eye level. Talk about the things that God made and the child's happiness in playing with the kittens.

Do It!

I'm a Little Seed

I'm a little, tiny seed
In the earth so low.
God sends sun and rain,
Then I start to grow.
Up, up, up,
Slowly I grow,
Then my leaves and flowers show!

ʃing It!

Animal Friends

(Tune: "Jingle Bells" chorus)

Oh, God made ducks
And rabbits and squirrels
And little birds to sing.
God made you and God made me.
Yes, God made everything!
(Repeat.)

Tell It!

God Made the World

God made everything that grows.
He made green grass
And pretty flowers grow on the ground.
He made trees grow way up high.
God made puppies grow into dogs
And kittens grow into cats.
Little pigs grow into big pigs and
Little cows grow into big
cows that say "moo!"
God made little babies grow bigger
And bigger—just like you.
(See Genesis 1:11-31.)

Display this poster at teacher's eye level in your nursery. Tell the Bible story, sing the song, do the finger play and repeat the Bible verse to one or more interested children.

Activities with Babies

Choose one or more of these learning activities to provide for babies during a session. Consider your facility, the number of babies and teachers and the supplies you have available as you plan which activities you will use. Continue the activity as long as the child is interested. For more information on using this curriculum, see "Why Use Curriculum?" on page 6.

God's Wonders

Big and Small

Collect

One or more nature items (pinecone, flower, apple, orange, small branch, potted plant)

Do

Look out a window or take a walk outside with a child and talk about the plants or trees. Describe the big and small things God has made: flowers, branches, rocks, etc.

Closely supervise as you let a child touch one or more nature items.

Say

Kendall, I see a big tree. God made the trees. I see a small leaf on the tree. God made the leaves. I'm glad God made all these big and small things.

Movement

God Made Me

Do

When you see a baby moving his or her arms or legs, talk about the baby's actions. Show pleasure as a baby succeeds in a physical action such as rolling over, crawling, etc.

Say

Isaiah, you are kicking your legs. God made your legs. God made you.

Julisa, you can roll over now! God made you, Julisa. God made everything that grows. Thank You, God, for making Julisa.

Music

Animals Grow

Collect

I Love to Sing! CD and player

One or more of these toy or stuffed animals: cat, dog, cow, pig, bird

Do

Play "Growing Things" while you are holding a baby. Show the toy or stuffed animals as mentioned in the song.

Move the animals in time to the music.

Say

Samuel, look at this little dog. God made puppies. They grow up to be dogs. Let's sing about the animals God made.

Thank You, God, for making animals that grow.

Tip

Use washable stuffed animals in your nursery. If a baby puts the stuffed animal in his or her mouth, set aside the animal to be washed.

God Made Animals

Collect

I Love to Sing! CD and player

April Bible Story Picture from *I Love to Look!* or *Nursery Posters*

Do

Show and talk about the picture. Play "Growing Things" and point to the animals.

Say

Here is a baby pig that says "oink, oink." Baby pigs grow to be big!

Brandon, you are growing to be bigger, too! God made everything that grows!

Pictures and Books

Touch and Feel

Collect

Sturdy books picturing animals with textured items to touch (or glue small fabric squares in a variety of textures to magazine pictures of animals and plants)

Do

Show pictures to a baby. As you talk about the picture, rub the baby's hand gently on the fabric.

Say

Angelina, here is a picture of a bunny. The bunny is soft. God made bunnies. Thank You, God, for bunnies.

Look, here's a picture of a dog. Can you feel the fur? God made dogs. God made everything that grows.

Animal Sounds

Collect

Sturdy books picturing a variety of animals

Do

Hold a baby in your lap and show him or her a picture in the book. Point to an animal, say its name and make the appropriate sound. Make the sound softer and then a little louder.

Repeat the conversation and animal sounds for other animals pictured in the book.

Say

Here is a cat. "Meow, meow" is the sound a cat makes. God makes cats. God made everything!

Victoria, do you see the cow? Cows say "moo, moo." I'm glad God made cows.

Quiet Play

Where Is My Bunny?

Do

While a baby is lying down or sitting in your lap, do the following finger play. Each time you repeat the rhyme, use other animals in the rhyme: kittens, puppies and birds.

Where is my little bunny?
No one can see.
I think my bunny is hiding from me.
Ah! There is my little bunny.
He's found a friend.
Look at all of them! There are ten!

Say

Chino, do you like bunny rabbits? God made little bunnies. God made you!

I'm glad for all the animals God made.

Tip

Babies will enjoy the sounds and actions, although they will not yet be able to do the actions.

Where Did It Go?

Collect

Several toy animals

Do

Get a baby's attention by showing him or her a toy animal. Talk about the animal and make its sound.

Hide the animal behind your back and ask, "Where did the cow go?" Then bring the animal out in front of you again saying, "Oh! Here's the cow. The cow says "moo, moo." Repeat the activity again, or give the animal to the child to hold.

Continue activity with other animals.

Say

Maya, God made the cow! God made all the animals.

Kyle, here is the elephant for you to hold. God made the elephant. God made you.

Activities with Toddlers

Choose one or more of the learning activities on pages 69-72 to provide for toddlers during a session. Consider your facility, the number of children and teachers and the supplies you have available as you plan which activities you will use. The best kind of teaching for toddlers will happen as you take advantage of teachable moments as children play and experience the learning activities you have provided. Continue an activity as long as one or more children are interested. For more information on using this curriculum, see "Why Use Curriculum?" on page 6.

Active Play

The Animals Walk

Do

Say, "Show me how a frog jumps. A frog uses its legs to jump like this." Encourage a child to pretend with you and jump.

Repeat the activity with other animals: rabbits hopping, birds flying, elephants stomping, kittens crawling.

Say

God made frogs. Noah, can you jump like a frog? God made all the animals. Thank You, God, for making frogs.

Tip

A child may want to repeat this activity several times. Or a child may not be interested the first time you invite participation, but may change his or her mind later on. Follow the child's lead.

Hide and Seek Animals

Collect

Several small stuffed animals

Do

Hide stuffed toy animals around the room. Make sure each animal is visible.

Ask a child to find a "hidden" animal. When an animal is found, identify it and lead child in making the appropriate animal sound.

Say

Ava, you found the bear! What sound does it make?

God made all the animals. God made animals to grow! I'm glad God made bears and rabbits and birds.

Fly Like a Bird

Collect

Several small scarves (or pieces of lightweight fabric)

Do

Hold a scarf in each hand. Wave scarves up and down to "fly like a bird." Give each child two scarves to wave up and down to "fly like birds."

Say

God made birds that grow. God made birds with wings so they can fly.

Dylan, I see that you are "flying" like a bird. Baby birds grow up to be mommy and daddy birds.

Obstacle Course

Collect

Items for simple obstacle course (cardboard box, large pillow, masking tape, toddler chairs, laundry basket, etc.)

Do

Set out items to make an obstacle course (box to walk around, pillow to crawl over, masking tape line to walk on, chairs to walk between, laundry basket to climb in and out of, etc.).

Move through the obstacle course yourself, and invite an interested child to follow you.

Say

Logan, you have grown to be so big! Look at all the things you can do. God planned for you to grow bigger and bigger!

God made everything that grows.

Art Play

Chalk Time

Collect

Sheets of paper
Jumbo chalk in several colors

Do

Put several pieces of chalk and several sheets of paper on a child-sized table.

Invite a child to draw with the chalk. You may draw a simple flower outline with a piece of chalk. Child may enjoy drawing on your flower shape.

Say

God made flowers. Brandy, do you see the petals on this flower? Do you want to use the red or yellow chalk?

Flowers grow. God made everything that grows. Thank You, God, for flowers.

Tip

If a child begins to put the chalk in his or her mouth, shake your head no and say, "The chalk doesn't taste good. We use the chalk to draw a picture." If a child continually puts the chalk in his or her mouth, gently remove the chalk and distract the child with a different activity or toy.

Soft Sheep

Collect

White paper plate for each child
Marker
Cotton balls
Glue sticks

Do

Draw a sheep face on each plate (see sketch). Give a paper plate to a child. Show him or her how to put glue on the plate and place a cotton ball on the glue. Child glues cotton balls onto plate.

Say

Chloe, here is a sheep face. You can glue some soft fur on the face. God made sheep. Sheep grow from little babies to grownup sheep.

You are growing, too! God made everything that grows.

God's Wonders

Hungry Animals

Note: Post a note alerting parents to the use of food. Also, check children's registration forms for possible food allergies.

Collect

Crackers and/or animal-shaped crackers

Do

When it's time for a snack, ask, "Are there any hungry cows here? Moo, moo, moo." Encourage a child to say "moo, moo." Give the child a cracker, saying, "Here's some food for these hungry cows."

Repeat the same activity, naming additional animals with which the child is familiar: pigs, horses, dogs, cats, birds, etc. Make the appropriate animal sounds and feed the hungry "animals" each time. If using animal-shaped crackers, talk about each animal shape.

Say

Darnel, I heard you meow just like a cat! God made cats. God made all the animals.

We're glad to have pets like dogs and cats. Thank You, God, for making animals.

Flowers Grow

Collect

Flowering plant on a tray
Small watering can with small amount of water in it

Do

Help each child have a turn to water the plant. (Optional: If possible in your location, take children outdoors to water plants.)

Say

God made the flowers. God gives them water and sunshine to help them grow.

God planned for you to grow, too!

Music

Ten Little Animals

Do

Hold up your fingers, one at a time, while you say the following rhyme, or sing the words to the tune of "Ten Little Children":

One little, two little, three little puppies.
Four little, five little, six little puppies.
Seven little, eight little, nine little puppies.
Ten little puppies say, "Woof, woof."

Repeat the rhyme, naming other animals familiar to young children and inserting the appropriate sounds.

Say

God made puppies. I'm glad God made puppies. Let's sing a song about puppies. Can you hold up your hands and show your 10 fingers?

What other animals did God make? God made kittens. God made everything that grows.

Look and Sing

Collect

I Love to Sing! CD and player
Unbreakable hand mirror

Do

Let a child look into a mirror while you play "God Made Grins." Name and point to the child's facial features.

Say

Connor, I see your big happy smile! God made you! God loves you and He is helping you to grow.

I'm glad God made my eyes. I'm glad God made my nose! God made us.

Pictures and Books

Cover-Up Game

Collect

Sturdy books pictures animals, plants and flowers

Do

While looking at a book with a child, point to a flower and say, "There is a flower." Then cover it with your hand and ask, "Where is the flower?" Uncover the item and announce, "Here is the flower!"
Repeat the game to  help the child enjoy anticipating discovery of each item.

Say

Braden, can you point to the sheep? God made sheep. God made everything that grows.

Tip

If you ask a child to respond in some way (pointing, making a sound, etc.), wait for the child to respond, but if he or she doesn't, simply do the action or make the sound yourself.

Who Made the Cows?

Collect

April Bible Story Picture from *I Love to Look!* or *Nursery Posters*

Do

Show and talk about the picture. Play a simple question and answer game with a child. Point to the cow and ask, "Who made the cows?" Briefly pause, and then say "God did!" Repeat several times with the animals pictured.

End the game by asking, "Who made Alexis?" Answer, "God did!"

Say

Animals grow. And people grow. Ethan, you are growing, too!

Pretend Play

Animals in the Barn

Collect

Several toy farm animals
Several sheets of brown, green and blue construction paper

Do

Put several toy animals on a sheet of brown paper (representing a barn). Also put sheets of green paper (grass) and blue paper (water) on the floor. Invite a child to play with you.

"Walk" one of the animals over to the green paper while saying, "This cow is hungry and wants to eat green grass." Then "walk" another animal from the barn to the blue paper. "Now this horse is thirsty and wants to drink cool water."

Continue playing with the animals, letting interested children play with the animals and moving the "barn," "grass" and "water" as desired.

Say

I see a cow and a horse inside the barn. The cow says "moo." The horse says "neigh." God made the animals.

Thank You, God, for making animals.

Animal Friends

Collect

Two or more animal puppets or washable stuffed animals

Do

Show the animals to a child. Ask the child to choose which animal he or she wants to be. Hold the remaining animal yourself, moving the animal and making appropriate animal sounds. Invite the child to move his or her animal and make animal sounds, too.

Continue as long as child is interested. If using puppets, be ready to help child put puppet on hand.

Say

Hailey, do you want to be the lamb or the duck? What does a lamb say? God made lambs.

God made all the animals. Animals grow, just like you! God made you.

Tip

Two children may want the same stuffed animal. Although a substitute animal may suffice, recognize that toddlers do not yet understand the idea of sharing. However, a toddler can begin to learn to take turns if guided gently, but firmly by an understanding adult.

Quiet Play

Stickers

Collect

Colored index cards
Animal or plant stickers

Do

Let children help you place a sticker on each card. Talk about the items pictured on the stickers.

Say

Torrie, you put a dog sticker on the card. God made dogs. Puppies grow to be dogs. Can you find a sticker of something else God made?

God made everything that grows. Let's see how many stickers we can find of things that grow.

Butterflies in the Air

Do

Hook your thumbs together and flutter your fingers like a butterfly. Fly the butterfly around the room, landing on various items and occasionally on a child. Talk about your actions. The child may wish to wave hands like a butterfly and fly his or her butterfly around the room.

Extend the activity by putting palms together and wiggling hands like a fish swimming.

Say

I'm pretending my hands are a butterfly. My butterfly is flying to the ball. Now my butterfly is flying over to Lily.

Aiden, God made butterflies. God made butterflies so they can fly. God made everything that grows.

May
People at Church Help Me

Jesus Helped His Friends
(See John 13:2-5.)

"God gives people to help me."
(See 1 Corinthians 12:28.)

This month you will help each child:
- develop an awareness of Jesus;
- associate Jesus with being loved and helped.

Devotional

Time in the nursery often seems a bit like a tornado: whoosh, children and parents suddenly arrive; fully absorbed, you whirl and turn and move through a series of caregiving tasks—then suddenly, they are gone! You sit breathlessly, assessing the needed cleanup and asking, "What on earth happened here?"

On such days, it may seem that one task after another took up all your time and energy. Was anything accomplished beyond basic physical care? In some nurseries, no more is expected. But Jesus shows us that in even the most ordinary act of care, there is potential for ministry. When Jesus washed His friends' feet, He taught them not only about being washed physically, but by the way in which He washed their feet, He also taught them the depth of His servanthood and the value He placed on each one of them—even the one who would betray Him. The disciples learned about servanthood and how Jesus valued each of them not by simply having their feet washed, but from the way in which it was done.

You are not merely a provider of services to children. You are a teacher! On the surface, those tasks may seem to involve only the physical care of changing diapers, feeding, playing, cuddling and singing. However, your actions go far beyond mere physical care and become ministry when you use them to express the warmth of Jesus' love. The gentle way in which you talk to, play with and love each child for whom you care teaches each of them something about Jesus' love and about the people at church who love God. That's a powerful lesson!

Such love will radiate from you only as you take time each day to "taste" God's goodness. As you consider His love for you and as you pray for each little one for whom you care, the routine tasks of service to children can become ministry!

During the month of May, display this poster at child's eye level. Talk about the way in which the adult in the poster is demonstrating God's love to the child by playing with him.

People at Church Help Me

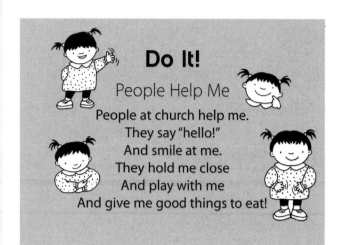

Do It!

People Help Me

People at church help me.
They say "hello!"
And smile at me.
They hold me close
And play with me
And give me good things to eat!

Sing It!

Showing God's Love

(Tune: "Twinkle, Twinkle, Little Star")

I will smile and play with you.
Jesus helped His good friends, too.
I can show I care for you
To help you know that God loves you.

Tell It!

Jesus Helped His Friends

One day Jesus and His friends
Walked and walked.
Their feet were very dirty!
So Jesus helped His friends.
He poured water into a big bowl.
Jesus washed His friends' feet
And dried them with a towel.
Jesus loved to help His friends.
People at church love to help you, too.
(See John 13:2-5.)

Display this poster at teacher's eye level in your nursery. Tell the Bible story, sing the song, do the finger play and repeat the Bible verse to one or more interested children.

Activities with Babies

Choose one or more of these learning activities to provide for babies during a session. Consider your facility, the number of babies and teachers and the supplies you have available as you plan which activities you will use. Continue the activity as long as the child is interested. For more information on using this curriculum, see "Why Use Curriculum?" on page 6.

God's Wonders

Bubble Fun!

Collect

Bubble-blowing solution and wand

Do

Blow bubbles in the nursery where a baby can see them. Point to the bubbles and talk about how they are floating around the room.

Gently blow a bubble toward a baby and describe the action.

Say

I'm blowing bubbles for you to see, William. I'm glad to be with you today.

I like taking care of you.

Movement

Up, Down and All Around

Collect

One or more baby rattles

Do

Stand near a baby who is in a crib, or sit near a baby who is lying on a blanket on the floor.

Shake a rattle directly in front of the baby. After the baby focuses on the rattle, move the rattle to a different location (up, down, side, behind your back) and shake it again.

Continue the activity as long as the baby is interested. When the baby indicates by movement or sound that he or she wants the rattle, give it to him or her.

Say

Madeline, can you hear the sound this rattle makes? I'll give you the rattle to play with. I'm glad to help you.

At church, people love to help you! We're glad you are here.

Music

Singing Time

Collect

I Love to Sing! CD and player

Do

When you are helping a baby (changing a diaper, putting on a jacket, feeding a bottle, bringing a toy, etc.), play "Helping."

You may also sing the following words to the tune of "Are You Sleeping?" Sing the child's name and appropriate pronoun in the song.

I love Lauren. I love Lauren. Yes, I do! Yes, I do!
I like to help her. I like to help her.
Yes, I do. Yes, I do.

Say

God loves you, Lauren. I love you, too. I'm glad to help you.

Thank You, God, for Lauren.

Tip

Let the baby know by your smile, your unhurried manner and your calm voice that you enjoy helping him or her.

I'll Smile at You

Collect

I Love to Sing! CD and player

Do

While you are holding, rocking or seated near

a baby, play "Yours and Mine." Make motions appropriate to the song (point to your mouth, point to child, etc.).

Say

James, I'm so glad you are here today. I like to be with you. I'm glad to help you.

At church, God gives us people who help us. God loves us.

Pictures and Books

My Favorite Toys

Collect

Sturdy book with pictures of familiar nursery toys

One or more toys similar to those pictured in the book

Do

Show a baby pictures of nursery toys. Show the child a similar toy in the nursery and compare it to the one in the picture.

Say

Michael, here is a picture of a ball. Look! Here is the ball we play with at church. God loves you, Michael.

It's fun to play together at church. I'll help you play with the ball.

Reading Together

Collect

Several sturdy picture books

Do

Offer two books to a child and let the child choose which one to read first. Continue as interest allows.

Say

Abby, I'm looking at this book about a farm. Would you like to look at the book with me? I'm glad to help you by reading a book with you.

Quiet Play

Silly Sounds

Do

Sit near a baby or hold him or her in your lap.

Make a silly sound (clicking tongue, animal sound, saying "la, la, la" or "boom, boom, boom"), repeating it several times in a row.

As long as the baby is interested, make additional sounds. Imitate any sounds the baby makes.

Say

We're playing by making silly sounds together. I'm glad to play with you.

Brianna, when you're at church I like to help you. Thank You, God, for Brianna.

Choose and Play

Collect

Two toys

Do

Place baby on a blanket on the floor. Bring two toys and sit with the child. While the child is watching you, do something with each toy (shake the rattle, tap the block, etc.).

Offer the child both toys. Watch to see which toy the child chooses and the way in which the child plays with the toys.

Say

Austin, I like to play with you. Look at these toys.

You're holding a block in each hand. I like to help you have toys to play with. Jesus loves you, Austin.

Tip

Repeating an action several times allows a child to focus on what you are doing.

Activities with Toddlers

Choose one or more of the learning activities on pages 77-80 to provide for toddlers during a session. Consider your facility, the number of children and teachers and the supplies you have available as you plan which activities you will use. The best kind of teaching for toddlers will happen as you take advantage of teachable moments as children play and experience the learning activities you have provided. Continue an activity as long as one or more children are interested. For more information on using this curriculum, see "Why Use Curriculum?" on page 6.

Active Play

Slide!

Collect
Several blocks
Sheet of cardboard
Several toy cars

Do
Stack several blocks on the floor. Lean a sheet of cardboard against the blocks to form a slide.
Invite a toddler to watch you as you let a car roll down the slide. Repeat the action several times.
Invite the child to play with the slide. Let the child experiment using the slide.

Say
Gracie, I'm going to let this car go down the slide. We're having fun playing with this slide.
I'm glad to help you by building the slide. I love you. God loves you, too.

Color Walk

Collect
4-inch (10-cm) construction paper squares in a variety of colors (red, blue, green, yellow)

Do
Give a child a red paper. Invite the child to walk around the room with you, looking for items the same color as the paper.
Repeat the activity with other colors.

Say
Jake, we're helping each other find red toys. God gives us people to love and help us. Thank You, God, for people who help us.

Row Boat

Do
Sit on the floor with a child as shown in the sketch.
Hold hands with the child and slowly rock back and forth, gently pushing and pulling the child's hands. (Optional: Sing "Row, Row, Row Your Boat" while rocking back and forth with child.)

Say
Jasmine, would you like to play row boat with me? Let's sit down on the floor together like this. We can hold hands and help each other go back and forth, back and forth.
I'm glad to play with you and help you. God loves you!

So High!

Collect
Blocks

Do
Invite a toddler to take turns with you building a block tower up to his or her shoulders.

Say
Brooke, let's build a tower together. We'll help each other!
Thank you for helping me. God gives us people to help us.

Art Play

Mother's Day Card

Collect

8½x11-inch (21.5x28-cm) sheet of white card stock for each child

Heart and flower stickers

Do

Fold sheet of card stock in half to make a card. Print "Happy Mother's Day" on front of card. Print "I'm glad God made you my mommy" on inside of card. Make a card for each child. (Optional: Instead of lettering each card individually, photocopy first card to make one card for each child.)

Children decorate cards with stickers.

Read the words to the child and write child's name inside card.

Say

This is a special card you can make to give to your mom. I will be glad to help you make your card.

I like to be with you at church, Adriana. Jesus loves you!

Tip

Participate with children in making a card yourself. A child will likely want to play and do what you do.

Foot Tracing

Collect

9x12-inch (23x30.5-cm) sheet of construction paper for each child

Jumbo crayons

Do

Show a child how you can trace around your foot on a sheet of paper.

Help a child stand on a sheet of paper while you use crayons to trace around the child's feet. Write the child's name on the paper.

Say

Let's make a drawing of your feet. I will help you! At church, people like to help you.

God's Wonders

Bags of Nature

Collect

Variety of nature items (shells, rocks, pinecones, leaves)

Several paper bags

Do

Children touch and examine the nature items, putting them in and out of the bags. Talk about the colors, sizes and textures of the items.

Encourage interested children to put all the shells in one bag, all the rocks in another bag, etc.

Say

Today we're looking at all these things that God made. I brought these things just for you to look at and touch.

Jesus liked to help His friends. I like helping you, too.

Bubble Fun!

Collect

Bubble-blowing solution and wand

Do

Blow bubbles in an open area of the room (or outdoors, if possible) where a child can see them and try to catch them. Point to the bubbles and talk about how they are floating around the room.

Gently blow a bubble toward a child and describe the action. Some children may want to try blowing through the wand while you hold the wand.

Say

I like to blow the bubbles for you to catch and pop! I like you, Sophie.

God gives people to help us. God loves us. Thank You, God, for people who help us.

Music

Circles and Squares

Collect

I Love to Sing! CD and player
Masking tape

Do

Use masking tape to make a large circle and square on the floor. (Remove tape after session ends.)

While playing "A Happy Place," walk with a child around the circle. Clap hands while you walk. Repeat the activity while walking around the square. (In another session, you can make these other shapes: triangle and zigzag.)

Demonstrate different ways of walking for a child to imitate if he or she chooses: walk on tip-toes, sliding, giant steps.

Say

Owen, we're walking around the circle. I'm glad to walk with you. And I'm glad to help you do new things.

God gives us people to help us. Thank You, God, for helpers.

Marching Band

Collect

I Love to Sing! CD and player
Rhythm instruments

Do

Let each child choose an instrument. Play "Helping" and march with children around the room.

Say

Let's be in a marching band together. Which instrument do you want? This is how you play it.

I like helping you at church. I'm glad you are here today.

Pictures and Books

Read with Me!

Collect

May Poster from *Nursery Smart Pages*
Sturdy picture books
Several large washable pillows

Do

Place books near pillows. Begin to look at a book, and invite an interested child to look at the book with you. Talk about the pictures. Point to the poster and talk about the teacher and boy playing together.

Say

Victoria, let's sit on the pillows and look at a book together. See the picture on the wall? That teacher is helping the little boy by playing with him. I like to help you, too.

When you are at church, people like to help you! God gives people to help you.

Who Helps You?

Collect

May Bible Story Picture from *I Love to Look!* or *Nursery Posters*

Do

Have the picture available as children are playing. When you help a child, or when you see a child help someone, be ready to show and talk about the picture.

Say

Fernando, thank you for handing the block to Gianna. You are a helper!

The Bible tells about a time Jesus helped His friends. He helped them by washing their feet.

Tip

While several toddlers may be interested in an activity at the same time, most of your "teaching" will happen one-on-one. Be ready to take advantage of teachable moments when you can connect the child's activity to the Bible theme.

Quiet Play

Puzzle Play

Collect

Several toddler puzzles

Do

Set out puzzles. Remove a piece from a puzzle, and let a child remove the other pieces. Describe what is pictured on the puzzle piece. Watch to see if the child can replace the puzzle piece. Help the child by setting a piece near the place where it belongs in the puzzle.

Say

Katie, look at this puzzle with all the animals. Let's help each other play with the puzzle. You can take out the pieces. We can help each other put them back.

I like to help you. God gives people to help you.

Tip

Don't rush to do the puzzle for the child. It takes many tries for a child to develop the skill required to complete a puzzle. One of the best ways to help a child develop that skill is to make large pieces with knobs on each piece.

Match the Picture

Collect

Sturdy game cards that have matching pictures

Do

Collect three or four pairs of cards. Set out one card from each pair. Show one of the matching cards to a child and let him or her find the matching card. Continue matching other cards if child is interested.

Say

Samuel, can you find the card that looks just like this one? It's fun to play this matching game. I like to help you play new games.

God gives people to help you. At church, I help you and Teacher Susan helps you. At home, your grandpa helps you.

Pretend Play

Going for a Walk

Collect

Dolls

At least one doll stroller or a large shoe box to which you have tied a string

Do

Place a doll in the stroller or in the shoe box. Pretend to take the doll for a "walk." Invite a child to take turn to help the doll go for a walk. Continue as long as the child is interested.

Say

Juan, I'm helping this doll go for a walk. Would you like a turn to be the helper? Thank you.

At church we can help each other. God loves us. God gives us people to help us.

Gettin' Ready to Eat

Collect

Toy dishes and cups
Several placemats

Do

Set out dishes, cups and placemats and use them to play with children. Let children pretend to serve you food and drink. Thank them for helping you and talk about the ways people help them.

Say

Elizabeth, I'm thirsty. Can you give me something to drink? Thank you. That milk tastes good. You are a helper! We can help each other.

Isaiah, who helps you have good food to eat at home? Your mom and dad help you. God gives us people to help us.

Thank You, God, for helpers.

June

God Cares for Me

Jesus Told About God's Care
(See Matthew 6:28-32.)

"God cares about you."
(See 1 Peter 5:7.)

• • • • • • • • • • • •

This month you will help each child:

• associate God with the loving care experienced at church;

• show interest in conversation and songs about God's care.

Devotional

It's easy to see how God could care for the young children in our care: sweet and happy, they delight us with their excitement over everyday things. It's a joy to tell them of His love as we play with them and care for them. No doubt God cares for them even more than we do! But what kind of care does God have for us grown-ups? Let's look at Peter's statement in 1 Peter 5:7: "Cast all your anxiety on him because he cares for you."

How much worrying do you think young children do? Do you suppose they wake in the morning, stressed over where their food will come from? Does their blood pressure rise as they fret over the possible problems of the day? Here they are, dependent on the caregivers—and instead of being stressed about their dependency, they respond in a blessed confidence, nestling in the arms of one who loves them and falling asleep in a relaxed lump of total trust. That's not just a sweet picture; it's the reality of God's care!

Now take a moment to think about the anxieties you faced this week: from the plumbing to the trouble your child had at school to worries about whether or not the groceries will stretch until payday. Adult lives seem to swell with stressful situations! Our blood pressure rises, our stomachs churn—and all the while, God invites us with open arms to give our anxieties to Him, relax in that child-like blessed confidence and stop losing sleep over our troubles! Perhaps we don't play with excitement as well as we once did, but God wants us to remember that no matter how big and responsible we are, we're still His little ones. He is willing—and waiting—to care for our anxiety. So give your anxieties to Him. Rest in Him. He cares for you!

During the month of June, display this poster at child's eye level. Talk about God's care for flowers and His wonderful love and care for children.

Do It!
God Cares for Me

God cares for me
When I sleep.
God cares for me
When I play.
God cares for me
All the time,
Every night and
Every day.

Sing It!
I'm So Glad

(Tune: "Skip to My Lou")

I'm so glad that God loves me, God
loves me, God loves me.
I'm so glad that God loves me, He loves
me all the time.
I'm so glad that God loves you, God
loves you, God loves you.
I'm so glad that God loves you, He loves
you all the time.

Tell It!
Jesus Told About God's Care

"Look at the pretty flowers,"
Jesus said.
"God makes them grow.
He makes red, yellow and white flowers.
God made these flowers,
And He cares for them.
God made you.
God loves you and cares for you, too.
God loves you even more than flowers."
(See Matthew 6:28-32.)

Display this poster at teacher's eye level in your nursery. Tell the Bible story, sing the song, do the finger play and repeat the Bible verse to one or more interested children.

Activities with Babies

Choose one or more of these learning activities to provide for babies during a session. Consider your facility, the number of babies and teachers and the supplies you have available as you plan which activities you will use. Continue the activity as long as the child is interested. For more information on using this curriculum, see "Why Use Curriculum?" on page 6.

God's Wonders

Flowering Plants

Collect

Small flowering plant

Do

Take a small flowering plant to a baby for a brief time of viewing (and careful touching).

Place plant out of reach when not being supervised.

Say

Look at this pretty flower. God cares for flowers and helps them grow.

God cares for you, too. God gives you food to eat and people to care for you.

Music

All the Time

Collect

I Love to Sing! CD and player

Do

Play "Twinkling Stars" while holding or rocking a baby. Sing along or hum the melody. Talk about God's care for the baby.

Say

Kaylie, God loves and cares for you all the time.

During the day when you are awake, God cares for you. During the night when you are sleeping, God cares for you. Thank You, God, for Your love and care.

Tip

Playing music can help you maintain a

relaxed, unhurried manner while you are giving a bottle to a baby. Continue to hold the baby for a few minutes after the feeding is finished. Quiet conversation and singing can make feeding a satisfying time.

Rhythm Fun

Collect

I Love to Sing! CD and player
Several rhythm instruments

Do

Play "All I Need." Shake a rhythm instrument in time to the music.

An older baby may want to hold the instrument. While the baby is holding the instrument, gently tap your fingers on the baby's leg, keeping time with the music.

Say

Christopher, God loves and cares for you. God gives you everything you need.

God gives you water to drink. God gives you applesauce to eat. God cares for you!

Movement

Baby Bounce

Do

Hold a baby so that only his or her feet touch your lap. Rhythmically lower and lift the child.

The baby may begin pushing his or her legs against you, bouncing up and down. Talk to the child while he or she is bouncing. Show your pleasure in his or her movement.

Say

Gavin, I can feel your legs pushing on my lap. You're bouncing up and down! I'm glad to play with you and take care of you.

God loves you!

Pictures and Books

God's Care

Collect

June Bible Story Picture from *I Love to Look!* or *Nursery Posters*
Flowering plant

Do

Show and talk about the picture, telling the brief story as he or she looks at a flowering plant.

Say

Look at this pretty flower. Jesus told a story about flowers. God cares for flowers. He gave them the rain and sunshine they need to grow.

God cares for you, too! God loves you, even more than flowers!

Tip

To use the picture from *Nursery Posters*, bring a baby to see the picture. Describe the items in the picture, pointing to each item as you talk about it.

Daytime and Nighttime

Collect

Sturdy book that shows daytime and nighttime pictures

Do

Look at the pictures in the book with a baby.

Look out a window or take a baby out doors, if possible, to see the blue sky and the sunshine.

Talk about how God cares for him or her during the daytime and the nighttime.

Say

Anna, can you see the sun in this picture? We can see the sun in the daytime. You like to play and eat during the day. God cares for you during the daytime.

During the night, we can see the stars and the moon. We sleep during the nighttime. God cares for you while you sleep.

Quiet Play

Fingers and Toes

Do

Repeat the following rhyme with a baby, touching the baby's fingers or toes as suggested by the words. Say the baby's name in place of the word "I."

Five fingers here, five fingers there.
Fingers I can use to play
All day long.

Five toes here, five toes there.
Toes I can use to wiggle
All day long.

Say

Zoey, God made your fingers and your toes. God cares for you!

I see your toes, Lucas. I see your fingers! God made you. Every day God cares for you.

Peekaboo Games

Collect

Small blanket or cloth
Doll or washable stuffed animal

Do

While facing a baby, partially cover your face with a blanket or cloth. Pause to let the baby observe you. Ask, "Where's Mrs. Smith?" Then pull the cloth off your head saying, "Peekaboo!" Repeat the game several times.

Place the cloth over the head of a doll or stuffed animal, and play the peekaboo game.

If the baby is interested, put the cloth on his or her head, letting it partially cover the baby's face. Then pull the cloth off as you say, "Peekaboo." An older baby may enjoy pulling the cloth off his or her own head.

Say

I'm glad to see you, Lydia. God loves you and cares about you!

Thank You, God, for Your love and care.

Activities with Toddlers

Choose one or more of the learning activities on pages 85-88 to provide for toddlers during a session. Consider your facility, the number of children and teachers and the supplies you have available as you plan which activities you will use. The best kind of teaching for toddlers will happen as you take advantage of teachable moments as children play and experience the learning activities you have provided. Continue an activity as long as one or more children are interested. For more information on using this curriculum, see "Why Use Curriculum?" on page 6.

Active Play

Walking, Walking, Stop!

Do

Walk with a child, holding his or her hand. While you are walking, say the following rhyme. When you say, "Stop!" help the child freeze in place with you. Then say the rhyme again, repeating the activity several times.

> We're walking, walking, walking.
> We're walking around our room.
> We're walking, walking, walking,
> But now we STOP!

With a child who is able to walk well, vary the activity with other motions: marching, moving arms as though swimming, or flapping arms as though flying.

Say

Evan, let's go for a fun walk together! Listen and do what I say.

I'm glad to see you're having fun, Evan. God cares for you!

Tug of War

Collect

Colorful bandanna

Do

Hold one end of a bandanna. Let a toddler hold the other end. Gently pull on the bandanna and talk about what you doing. Wait for the child to pull back on the bandanna.

Continue taking turns pulling on the bandanna.

Say

I'm pulling on this cloth. Can you pull, too? Isabelle, now you are pulling on the cloth. You have strong hands.

It's fun to play together. God cares about you when you are playing. God cares about you all the time.

Block Road

Collect

Cardboard or wooden blocks

Toy cars and trucks

Do

Outline a road with the blocks for a toddler to walk on.

Allow the child time to experiment walking on the block road. Each time the child walks on the road, name a pretend destination at the end of the road (store, park, church, etc.).

Child may also move toy cars and trucks on the block road.

Say

Liam, you're walking on the road. I think you are going to the park to play. God cares for you at the park.

Let's drive these cars on the road. Where should the cars go? I think they are going to church. God cares for you at church. God cares for you all the time!

Tip

Observe how children use the toys in your room. Are the toys the kind that can be used in a variety of ways? Or do children merely pick them up, look at them and drop them? Remove those toys that children seem to ignore. In a month or so, bring them out again to see if children will use them more purposefully.

Wading Pool

Collect
Small empty inflatable or plastic wading pool
Several child-safe pool toys

Do
Let a child climb in and out of the pool. Allow time for the child to sit in the pool and play with the toys. Talk about God's care for the child.

Say
Alexandra, I see that you are in the pool. Do you like to play in the water? God gives people to take good care of you in the water.

God cares for you every day. Thank You, God, for Your love and care.

Art Play

"God Cares for Me" Picture

Collect
12x18-inch (30.5x45.5-cm) sheet of construction paper for each child
Marker
Magazine pictures of people and food
Glue sticks

Do
Print the words "God cares for me" on each paper. Help one child at a time glue pictures onto the paper.

Say
These words say, "God cares for me." Casey, do you see the picture of this mom? God gave you a mom because He cares for you. You can glue this picture on your paper.

Paige, what picture do you want to glue on to your paper? God gives you food like apples. God cares for you.

Father's Day Card

Collect
8½x11-inch (21.5x28-cm) sheet of card stock or construction paper for each child, folded in half
Marker
Stickers
Jumbo crayons

Do
Write "I love you, Daddy" or other greeting inside the card. Write the child's name.

Encourage child to decorate the card with stickers and coloring.

If a child is interested, trace child's hand with crayon.

Say
Would you like to make your daddy (uncle, grandpa, etc.) a card?

We can put your handprint on the front.

Your daddy cares for you. God cares for you, too!

God's Wonders

Flower Vases

Collect
Fresh or artificial flowers
Several large plastic cups

Do
Set out the flowers and cups. Invite children to touch and smell the flowers.

Children may also arrange the flowers in the plastic-cup vases. Talk with children about the colors and feel of the flowers.

Say
God made the flowers. God cares for the flowers by giving them sunshine and water.

Carson, God cares for you. God shows His love to you every day. Thank You, God, for Your love and care.

God's Wonders

What's in the Bag?

Collect

Variety of 4-inch (10-cm) fabric squares in different colors and textures
   Bag

Do

One at a time, place a fabric square into the bag.
   Children take turns looking into the bag and then taking out the fabric square.

Say

Vanessa, you used your eyes to look into the bag. Then you used your hand to take the red cloth out of the bag. God made your hands. God cares for you!

Music

Hear Me Sing!

Collect

I Love to Sing! CD and player
   Half circle of construction paper folded and taped into megaphone shape; optional—plastic megaphone

Do

Play "All I Need" and sing or speak the echo portion of the song while holding the megaphone up to your mouth.
   As the child becomes interested, hold the megaphone for the child to talk through or let the child hold the megaphone.

Say

Hi, Maria! God loves you. God cares about you.
   God gives us good food to eat like bananas. God gives us good things to drink like milk. God loves us!

   Tip

Make paper megaphone for each child. If using a plastic megaphone, wash and disinfect the megaphone after a child has used it.

Circle Walk

Collect

I Love to Sing! CD and player

Do

Play "I See You!" and do the actions described in the song.
   If a child is interested, hold the child's hands and walk in a circle as you sing the song.

Say

God cares about you, Jillian. God made your feet. God made your hands. God gives you just what you need.
   We can thank God for His care. Thank You, God!

Pictures and Books

Flower Gardens

Collect

June Poster from *Nursery Posters*

Do

Display the poster at child's eye level. Describe the items and people in the poster. Invite a child to point to various items in the poster. Talk about God's love and care.

Say

Juliana, I see lots of flowers in this picture. Can you point to the flowers? I see a little girl. Can you point to the girl? What is she doing?
   God cares for flowers by giving them sunshine and rain to help them grow. God cares for you, too. God gave you people to love you. God wants you to have the things that you need to grow.

Surprise Pictures

Collect

June Bible Story Picture from *I Love to Look!*; optional—similarly-sized magazine pictures of families, flowers and trees and food
   Manila envelope slightly larger than the Bible Story Picture Card

Do

Insert the picture(s) inside the envelope. While the child is watching, slowly remove the picture from the envelope. Identify and describe the items in the picture.

Say

Riley, watch to see what is on this picture. What do you see? I see yellow and red flowers. I see two children. And look, there is Jesus. Jesus told a story about flowers. Jesus said that God cares for flowers. Jesus said that God cares for you, even more than flowers.

Pretend Play

My House!

Collect

Blanket or sheet
Sturdy card table
Doll and doll blankets
Toy dishes and cups

Do

Put a blanket or sheet over a table, leaving one side completely open, to create a "house" for a child to play in. Place a doll, several doll blankets and play dishes in the house.

Invite a toddler to play in the house, caring for the doll.

Say

Cade, I think your baby is hungry. What can you give him to eat? You have a daddy who takes good care of you. God cares for you, too.

Quiet Play

What's in the Cup?

Collect

Several small toys (too large to be swallowed)
Several paper or plastic cups

Do

Place a small toy in each of the cups. Then ask, "What's in these cups?" Slowly take the toys in and out of the cups several times, identifying

the toys and saying "in" and "out" at the appropriate times.

Say

Taylor, I like playing with you. I like to take care of you. God cares for you and loves you, too.

Where Are You?

Do

Pretend that you cannot see a toddler. Say, "Where is Cameron? I can't see him!" Pretend to look all around for the child. Talk about the places you look.

Then look directly at the child and smile as you say "Oh, there's Cameron."

Repeat the activity several times, each time pretending to look for the child in different places.

Say

God cares about you, Cameron. God cares about you all the time!

One, Two, Three! God Loves Me!

Collect

Rhythm instrument (shaker, bells, etc.)

Do

While seated near a toddler, shake a rhythm instrument as you say these words:

One and two. God loves you.
One, two, three. God loves me.

Repeat the words and actions several times.

Say

Joseph, I'm glad God loves you. I'm glad God loves me.

Thank You, God, for loving us.

July
God Made Me

God Made Everything
(See Psalm 95:3-7.)

"God made me."
(See Job 33:4.)

• • • • • • • • • • •

This month you will help each child:

• enjoy success in using the body God made for him or her;
• begin to develop an awareness that God made his or her body.

Devotional

Perhaps Adam felt like a child with a new toy when the Lord brought the animals for him to name. What an array of creatures! All shapes, sizes, colors—each one was uniquely fascinating, deserving of extended scrutiny. Imagine Adam's delight as he first stroked the lion's mane, admired a peacock as its tail fanned out, observed a monkey's antics. Yet even as Adam delighted in each new form of life, God was aware that none of these creatures could ever be a suitable companion for Adam. Only another human could meet Adam's wide range of needs and interests.

Every descendant of Adam and Eve carries the same need for human companionship. While the child's intense curiosity can be satisfied with toys, pictures, books and animals, contact with people remains his or her overpowering interest. Just as God recognized Adam's need, adults who care for young children must recognize that each child needs the companionship of a caring person. Meeting that need calls for giving more than bottles or crackers. It requires patient and understanding adults who give themselves willingly to the task of showing God's love to each of His little ones.

During the month of July, display this poster at child's eye level. Describe what the child in the poster is doing and how God's love is shown in the way He made us.

Do It!

God Made

God made my ears.
God made my nose.
God made my fingers.
God made my toes.
God made my eyes.
They're both open wide.
God made my mouth
With a tongue inside!

Sing It!

I Have Two Eyes

(Tune: "Pop Goes the Weasel")

I have two eyes.
I have two ears.
I have two hands and feet.
I have one mouth
And one little nose,
But, oh, so many fingers and toes!

Tell It!

God Made People

God made everything!
God made the cold water we drink.
God made the big waves in the sea.
God made the land that's all around us.
God made all the people, too—
Big ones and little ones,
People like me, and people like you.
God made us. And we are glad!
(See Psalm 95:3-7.)

Display this poster at teacher's eye level in your nursery. Tell the Bible story, sing the song, do the finger play and repeat the Bible verse to one or more interested children.

Activities with Babies

Choose one or more of these learning activities to provide for babies during a session. Consider your facility, the number of babies and teachers and the supplies you have available as you plan which activities you will use. Continue the activity as long as the child is interested. For more information on using this curriculum, see "Why Use Curriculum?" on page 6.

God's Wonders

Who Do You See?

Collect

Unbreakable mirror (hand mirror, or mounted on wall)

Do

Sit or stand near a mirror while holding a baby. Ask, "Who do you see?" Say, "I see Jessica."

Describe the parts of the baby's body you can see in the mirror, touching each body part (eyes, nose, ears, hands, etc.) as you talk about it.

Say

Jessica, I see your brown eyes. God made your eyes. God made you.

I see your hands, Jessica. You have five fingers on this hand, and five fingers on your other hand. God made your hands. Thank You, God, for Jessica's hands.

Movement

Roll Over

Collect

Small rattle or other baby toy

Do

Lay a baby on his or her back. Sitting behind the baby's head, hold a small rattle or toy above the baby's face.

Once you have the baby's attention, slowly move the rattle or toy over to one side, encouraging the baby to grab for it. Wait to see if the baby turns over. Give the baby the rattle or toy after he or she turns over, or if the baby expresses interest in holding the rattle or toy.

Describe what the baby is doing.

Say

Julian, you can see the toy I'm holding. God made your eyes so you can see.

You rolled over, Joshua, so you can reach the toy. God made your body to do so many things.

Music

Here I Am

Collect

I Love to Sing! CD and player
Doll

Do

Play "Here I Am" to a baby while you are holding a doll.

Point to the body parts of the doll according to the words of the song.

Say

Thank You, God, for making Jordan. Thank You for Jordan's hands. Thank You for Jordan's feet.

God made us. God loves us.

Wave and Wave

Collect

I Love to Sing! CD and player
Several bandannas or scarves

Do

Play "We're Special" and wave a bandanna or scarf in time to the music. Hold the bandanna or scarf near a baby. Let the baby grab the scarf if he or she is interested.

Continue playing song and waving your bandanna or scarf.

Say

Savannah, you're holding onto the scarf with your hand. God made your hands.

God made every part of you. God loves you.

Tip

Softly playing the songs on *I Love to Sing!* can help maintain an even sound level in the nursery, making napping easier for babies.

Pictures and Books

Baby Books

Collect

Sturdy picture books about babies

Do

Look at a book with a child. Connect what the child is seeing to this month's theme: God Made Me.

For example, point to a child's ears in a picture. Say, "Here are the baby's ears." Then place your hands on the child's ears as you say, "Here are your ears."

Say

Travis, here are your ears. God made your ears. God made you.

I'm glad that God gave us ears so we can hear.

God Made the World

Collect

July Bible Story Picture from *I Love to Look!* or *Nursery Posters*

Sturdy books that picture nature scenes (flowers, oceans, mountains, trees, etc.)

Do

Show and talk about the Bible story picture. Let a child look at pictures in books, too.

Pont out several things God made such as a tree, grass, birds or other people.

Say

The Bible tells us that God made you and God made me. God made so many wonderful things!

Every day we can see wonderful things that God has made.

Tip

If you have an outdoor play area and the appropriate number of teachers for supervision, take a baby outdoors when possible. Tell the brief Bible story for this month while you are outside. Point to the appropriate items.

Quiet Play

My Face

Collect

Paper plate

Marker

Stapler

Fabric or paper piece large enough to cover plate

Do

Draw a face on the plate. Staple a piece of fabric or paper at the top of the face to cover it.

When you are near a baby, lift up the covering to show the face. Talk about the eyes, nose and mouth on the face.

Say

Look, Miles, here's a face. I see two eyes. I see a nose. I see a mouth. You have two eyes, a nose and a mouth, too. God made all of you!

God loves you.

Touch and Feel Balls

Collect

Variety of balls in different sizes and textures

Do

Set out two balls and let babies explore how the balls feel.

Describe the texture of the ball as a baby touches it.

Say

Logan, you are touching the soft ball. Here is a different ball; it feels smooth. God made your fingers to touch.

God loves you and made your body just right.

Activities with Toddlers

Choose one or more of the learning activities on pages 93-96 to provide for toddlers during a session. Consider your facility, the number of children and teachers and the supplies you have available as you plan which activities you will use. The best kind of teaching for toddlers will happen as you take advantage of teachable moments as children play and experience the learning activities you have provided. Continue an activity as long as one or more children are interested. For more information on using this curriculum, see "Why Use Curriculum?" on page 6.

Active Play

Cardboard Hills

Collect

Large sheet of cardboard (or poster board)
Toy cars or trucks

Do

Fold cardboard or poster board in half and stand it up on the floor to make a "hill."

Hold a car or truck at the top of the hill. Count "one, two, three." Then release the car or truck so that it rolls down the hill. Invite the child to imitate your actions.

The child will also enjoy moving the cars and trucks through the tunnel formed by the cardboard.

Say

I'm glad we have hands to play with. God made your hands, Kylie.

God made us so we can do many things.

Tip

Avoid pressuring a child to always play with a toy "the right way" or the way that you have planned. Experimentation is necessary and satisfying. Simply affirm the child's efforts as you talk about the skills he or she has developed.

Music to My Ears

Collect

Wind-up toy that makes music or child-safe kitchen timer

Do

Wind up the toy or set the kitchen timer. Tell a

child that you are going to hide the item. Hide the item behind an object in the room.

Ask the child to find the item and bring it back to you. Repeat the activity as long the child is interested.

Say

Elton, you found the timer! Hearing the ticking sound helped you find the toy. God made your ears so you can hear.

What else can we hear in our room today? We can hear people talking. We can hear music. I'm glad God made our ears.

Ball Play

Collect

Several balls

Do

Set the balls on the floor (outdoors in a toddler playground, if possible).

Play with the balls, using your hands and feet. Hold a ball, drop a ball, toss a ball, roll a ball and tap a ball with your feet. Invite children to play with balls, too.

Say

Dylan, you used your hands to drop the red ball. God made your hands. Can you use your foot to kick the ball? God made your feet. God loves you!

Thank You, God, for making our hands and feet.

Paint with Water

Collect

Several large, soft paintbrushes
Pail of water

Do

Bring children outdoors to a toddler playground. Let a child use a paintbrush to "paint" the sidewalk or buildings with water.

Talk about how the color of various objects changes when child is painting.

Say

Terrell, you are using your hand to paint. Now use your eyes to watch what happens when you paint. God made your hands. God made your eyes.

God made you and God made me. God made so many wonderful things.

Art Play

Collage

Collect

Colorful fabric and/or paper scraps about 2 inches (5 cm) square

Glue sticks

Construction paper sheet for each child

Do

Let children glue fabric and/or paper scraps onto paper. Demonstrate how to rub glue onto paper and place fabric or paper on top.

Say

Molly, you are gluing the blue paper. I see a red paper, too. God made your eyes to see colors.

Sean, you are using your hands to glue the papers. God made your hands.

God made us! He made us just right!

Tip

Have the supplies for activities collected before the session begins. Once children arrive, teachers cannot leave to gather supplies.

God's Wonders

Texture Walk

Collect

Variety of textured fabrics or materials (silk, towel, plastic mat, wool, corduroy)

Do

Set out fabrics and materials to make a path on which children may walk. Remove children's shoes and socks so they can walk barefoot on the path. If it is not possible to remove shoes and socks, children feel the path with their hands.

Encourage children to feel the differences in the fabrics and materials. Describe what children are feeling.

Say

Eduardo, you are walking on the shiny blue cloth. It feels soft and smooth. God made your feet. God loves you!

We can do so many things! God made us in such a wonderful way.

Bag It!

Collect

Nature objects (rock, seashell, pinecone, etc.)

Bag

Do

One at a time, hand each object to a toddler. Talk about how each object feels and say the object's name. Put the objects into a bag.

Ask the child to reach into the bag and take out one of the objects.

Say

Zoey, what do you feel? Show me what you found in the bag. You felt the seashell with your hands. God made your hands. God made you!

God made your hands so you could play. God made your hands so you could do many things.

I Can Taste

Note: Post a note alerting parents to the use of food. Also, check children's registration forms for possible food allergies.

Collect

Variety of finger foods such as O-shaped cereal, raisins, small pieces of cheese, etc.

Napkins and small plates

Do

Give children a variety of foods to taste. Talk about the foods' characteristics (sweet, salty, crunchy, etc.).

Say

These raisins are sweet. God made your mouth to taste and eat good food. Thank You, God, for making our mouths.

I'm glad God made you.

Music

Hat Parade

Collect

I Love to Sing! CD and player
Several plastic or washable hats

Do

Play "Here I Am!" and invite a child to walk with you around the room. Several interested children might join in to form a parade.

Provide hats for children to wear if they choose while parading around the room.

Say

Darnel, here's a firefighter hat you can wear on your head. God made your head! God loves you.

Lily, this songs talks about your head. Can you pat your head? Where is your foot? Can you point to your foot? God made every part of you.

Pat the Drum

Collect

I Love to Sing! CD and player
Empty food containers suitable for drums

Do

Ask child to select a container for his or her drum. Talk about the food that came in the container.

Children tap drums with hands while listening to "God Made Me" on CD.

Say

Let's listen to some music and play the drums. God made your hands so you can play the drums.

God made you. Thank You, God, for making Maggie.

Tip

Once you have demonstrated how to tap the drums, sit back and observe how the child experiments with the drums.

Pictures and Books

Animal Sounds

Collect

Sturdy books with pictures of animals

Do

Show a child the animal pictures. Point to the animals, say its name and make the appropriate animal sound. Ask the child to make the sound, too.

Say

Annie, you made the sound of a cat. We can make sounds like these animals.

God made our mouths so we can sing and talk. I'm glad God made us.

I Can Play!

Collect

July Poster from *Nursery Posters*
Sturdy books picturing children playing (using their hands, arms, legs and feet in a variety of ways)

Do

Show pictures to children and talk about what the children are doing. Connect what the child is seeing to this month's theme: God Made Me.

For example, point to a child's legs in a picture and then gently touch the child's legs as you talk about God making our legs.

Say

Isaac, can you point to the boy's hands? Here are your hands. You can use your hands to play with balls, just like this boy is doing.

God made your hands. God made you.

Pretend Play

Telephone Talk

Collect

Toy telephone

Do

While a toddler is playing, hold a play telephone.

Pretend to make the phone ring. Pick up the phone and talk, describing the different ways in which the child is playing.

Let the child have a turn to talk on the telephone, too.

Say

Ashley is playing with blocks today. She's using her hands to build with blocks. She is using her eyes to see the blocks.

God made Ashley. God made her hands and God made her eyes.

Quiet Play

Upside Down

Collect

Several toys

Do

Sit with a toddler on the floor.

Place several toys upside down on the floor. Say, "This car is upside down. This camera is upside down, too."

Watch to see what the child does. If the child places the toys right side up, or places other toys upside down, describe the child's actions.

Say

Brady, I can see that you like to put the toys upside down! It's fun to play with toys. God made your hands so you can play.

Jenna, you've put the toys back on the shelf. Thank you! You used your hands to clean up the toys. God made your hands to do many things.

Tip

Your acceptance and encouragement of the manner in which a child plays helps a child develop confidence for further learning and exploration.

Paper Surprises

Collect

Several small toys

Variety of papers: construction paper, wrapping paper, tissue paper, aluminum foil

Tape

Do

Tape a sheet of paper around a toy. Feel the wrapped toy with your hands and say, "I wonder what toy surprise is in this paper."

Then let a child feel the wrapped toy. Help the child undo the paper to find the surprise toy.

Wrap another toy and repeat the activity.

Say

Austin, God made your hands so you can feel this toy. God made you.

You are using your eyes to look at the surprise. God made your eyes. God made every part of you. Thank You, God.

My Doll and I

Collect

Doll

Do

Compare a doll's features with those of a child.

Point to the doll's nose, the child's nose and then your nose. Identify your actions with words.

Ask a child to play this pointing game with you.

Say

Mackenzie, here is the doll's nose. Here is your nose. And here is my nose! God made your nose. God made you. God made me, too.

I'm glad God made us. I'm glad God loves us.

August

God Gives Me Friends

David and Jonathan Were Friends
(See 1 Samuel 18:1-4.)

"Love each other."
(See John 15:12.)

This month you will help each child:

• enjoy happy encounters with other children at church;

• associate God with happy experiences at church.

Devotional

Take some time to read the story of David and Jonathan's friendship found in 1 Samuel 18—19:7. Notice how the circumstances of David and Jonathan's friendship changed drastically. At first, everything seemed rosy. Jonathan, King Saul, Saul's servants and all the people liked David. Friendship flourishes easily when things are going well.

But by the beginning of chapter 19, Saul's love for David has turned to raging jealousy. Now Saul seeks to turn Jonathan against David. Here comes the test of true friendship. Braving the wrath of his father the king, Jonathan stands up for his friend. It would have been so easy to bend, but Jonathan stood firm in the face of enormous pressure.

How strong are the friendships among the staff in your department? Are you merely acquaintances who happen to work together in the same room? Are you easily compatible only as long as everything runs smoothly? Or have you built relationships that help you sustain each other when pressure comes?

As you teach young children about friendships, nurture your relationships with the others who work with you. Pray for them, asking God's Spirit to knit your hearts together as He did the hearts of David and Jonathan.

During the month of August, display this poster at child's eye level. Talk about the way in which the children in the poster are showing that they are friends.

Do It!

I Roll the Ball

I roll the ball to you.
You roll the ball to me.
I can share the ball with you
Because we're friends, you see!

Sing It!

Friends

(Tune: "Farmer in the Dell")

We can smile and wave.
We can smile and wave.
Because it's fun to be with friends,
We can smile and wave.

Tell It!

David and Jonathan Were Friends

David and Jonathan were friends.
They played like good friends do.
They helped each other, too.
Jonathan gave David his coat.
Jonathan said, "I love you."
"Thank you, Jonathan," David
said, "I love you, too."
God gives us friends, and we are glad.
(See 1 Samuel 18:1-4.)

Display this poster at teacher's eye level in your nursery. Tell the Bible story, sing the song, do the finger play and repeat the Bible verse to one or more interested children.

Activities with Babies

Choose one or more of these learning activities to provide for babies during a session. Consider your facility, the number of babies and teachers and the supplies you have available as you plan which activities you will use. Continue the activity as long as the child is interested. For more information on using this curriculum, see "Why Use Curriculum?" on page 6.

God's Wonders

Sea Shells

Collect

Several sea shells too large to swallow

Do

Hold a shell in your hand. Let a baby look at it. Take the baby's hand and gently touch a shell with it.

Say

Look at these shells God made. Braden, I'm glad you came to play today.

We are with our friends. God gives us friends.

Movement

Playing Together

Collect

Light piece of fabric or doll blanket

Do

Sit facing a sitting baby on the floor. Put the fabric or blanket on top of the baby's hands. Say, "Where are your hands?" When the baby moves his or her hands out again, say, "There are your hands!"

Play this game several times, occasionally covering up one of your hands, too. Also play this game by putting the fabric or blanket on top of the baby's feet. Let the child move his or her feet out from under the blanket.

Say

Madison, let's play together. I'm glad to be your friend and play with you.

God gives us friends. Friends love each other.

Music

See My Friends?

Collect

I Love to Sing! CD and player

Do

Play "Friends." While the music is playing, hold a baby and walk around the room and saying the names of the other children or teachers in the room.

If you are seated on the floor, point to other children or teachers at appropriate times in the song.

Say

Zoey, we're singing about our friends. We're glad to see our friends.

Look, there is your friend Madison and Lily. And here is your friend Ben. God gives you friends.

Tip

When singing songs at church, insert a child's name into the songs wherever possible. Many babies learn to recognize their names in conversation and songs. Occasionally touch the child as you sing, to help the child associate the name with him- or herself.

Clapping Song

Collect

I Love to Sing! CD and player

Do

Play "My Friends." Clap your hands while listening to this song with a baby. Gently touch the child's hands together several times, too.

Say

James, I'm glad when you smile. You are my friend!

When we come to church, we see our friends. Thank You, God, for our friends at church.

Pictures and Books

Two Friends

Collect

August Bible Story Picture from *I Love to Look!* or *Nursery Posters*

Do

Show and talk about the Bible story. Point to the people in the picture and say their names.

Say

Kyla, here is a picture of two friends. This is David and this is Jonathan. They loved each other. They helped each other.

God gives us friends, too. We can love and help our friends.

Friendly Children

Collect

Sturdy books picturing babies and toddlers

Do

Show a baby the pictures in a book. If a baby is laying in a crib, open the book and set it up approximately 10 to 12 inches (25.5 to 30.5 cm) from the baby's face. Occasionally, open the book to a different page. Talk about what the baby sees.

You may also hold a baby in your lap and look at the pictures together.

Say

Thomas, look at the pictures of the children in this book. Here's a baby who is sleeping. This baby is playing with a ball.

I like looking at books with you. You are my friend. I'm glad you came today to be with your friends. God gives us friends.

Tip

Be alert to signs that a baby is tired or sleepy.

Some babies resist taking a nap in strange surroundings. Reading a book together may calm the baby down so that he or she can relax enough to fall asleep.

Quiet Play

Getting to Know You

Do

Sit holding a baby securely so that he or she can look at and touch your face.

Smile and talk to the baby. If the baby touches a part of your body—hand, chin, etc.—talk about the baby's actions.

Responding to the sounds and actions of the baby will encourage the baby to initiate further interaction.

Say

Jamie, you touched my chin! You're my friend. I'm glad we are friends.

God gives us friends. Friends love each other.

Round and Round

Collect

Brightly-colored toy

Do

Bring a brightly-colored toy and stand or sit near a baby. When the baby has focused on the toy, slowly move it in a circle as you say the following rhyme:

Round and round we go.
Round and round we go.
Round and round we go. Touch the baby's toes!

On the last line of the game, touch the toy to the child's toes. Repeat game several times, changing the word "toes" to "nose" and touching the child's nose.

Say

Sydney, I like to play with you. You are my friend.

God gives us friends. It's fun to play with our friends.

Activities with Toddlers

Choose one or more of the learning activities on pages 101-104 to provide for toddlers during a session. Consider your facility, the number of children and teachers and the supplies you have available as you plan which activities you will use. The best kind of teaching for toddlers will happen as you take advantage of teachable moments as children play and experience the learning activities you have provided. Continue an activity as long as one or more children are interested. For more information on using this curriculum, see "Why Use Curriculum?" on page 6.

Active Play

Down the Road

Collect
Masking tape
Several toy cars and toy people

Do
Make several masking-tape roads (and at least one intersection) on the floor. (Remove tape after session ends.)

"Drive" a toy car on the road. Then let the child have the car. If the child is interested, say "Drive your car on the roads and I'll make my car follow yours." Then follow the turns and stops that the child makes with his or her cars.

This activity can be repeated with toy people who you "walk" down the road.

Say
Bailey, I like to play cars with you. It's fun to be at church with you. God gives us friends to have fun with.

We love our friends. Thank You, God, for our friends.

Beanbag in the Baskets

Collect
Several beanbags
Laundry basket
Small basket

Do
Let children toss or drop beanbags into the baskets. Children may also take beanbags in and out of the baskets.

Talk about which basket is big, and which basket is small.

Say
Anthony, you put the beanbag into the big basket. And Maggie put her beanbag into the small basket.

Anthony and Maggie are friends. They like to play together.

God gives us friends. I see lots of friends in this room.

Crawl Through the Tunnel

Collect
Fabric tunnel or large cardboard box with ends cut off
Brightly-colored toy

Do
Set out the tunnel or box. Show the toy to a child and then place the toy inside the tunnel or box. An interested child may crawl inside the tunnel or box to get the toy.

Some children may crawl all the way through the tunnel or box, while others will enjoy sitting inside.

Say
Cameron, you crawled inside the tunnel. So did Kenna! It's fun to play with our friends.

God gives us friends. Friends love and help each other.

Smile and Wave

Do
While you are standing near one or two children, say and do the motions for the following rhyme:

We can smile and wave.
We can smile and wave.
Because it's fun to be with friends,
We can smile and wave.

Repeat the rhyme several times, encouraging children to do the motions, too. Then lead interested children on a "smiling and waving" march around the room while you say the rhyme.

Say

God gives us friends. We have fun with our friends. We love our friends.

Art Play

Paper Plate Puppets

Collect

Paper plates
Jumbo crayons

Do

Draw happy faces on plates.

Children may color on the plates. Make two plates for yourself.

Hold up two paper plates and use them like puppets. Have the puppets talk to each other. For example, one puppet may say, "Hello! Will you be my friend?" The other puppet may answer, "Yes, I'll be your friend."

Say

We're making puppets with our friends today. God gives us friends.

Crayon Play

Collect

Sheet of butcher paper
Tape
Jumbo crayons

Do

Tape paper to a child-sized table. Invite a toddler to join you at the table.

Draw a line on the paper. Continue drawing lines. Let the child draw lines and other marks.

Say

Justin, I like to color with you.
I'm glad God gave me friends like you!

Tip

Toddlers most often play alongside each other, rather than playing "with" each other. Coloring on the same large sheet of paper will help them start to interact with each other.

God's Wonders

What Do You Hear?

Collect

Rhythm instruments such as bells and shakers, or two small blocks

Do

Make an interesting sound for a child to hear (ring a bell, use the shaker, tap the blocks together). Ask, "Can you hear the sound the bell made?" Let the child have a turn to make the sound.

Continue the activity with other sounds (knocking on wall, patting on a table, etc.).

Say

We're listening to sounds together. You're my friend. God gives us friends.

We can love and help our friends.

Friends at Play

Collect

Sand shovels and pails

Do

Bring children outdoors to a sand play area.

Children play with sand toys.

Say

Julian, you are playing in the sand with your friends today. What are your friends' names?

God gives us friends to play with. I see lots of friends here today. I see Julian, and Victoria and Sophie.

Music

Sing and Play

Collect

I Love to Sing! CD and player
Several balls

Do

Play "My Friends" as you roll a ball to a child. Say the name of the child as you roll the ball to him or her. Encourage the child to roll the ball back to you or another child. (A toddler may prefer to keep the ball and carry it around.)

Say

Olivia, I am rolling a ball to you. Now I'm rolling a ball to Devin. We're playing with our friends.

I'm glad for our friends at church. God gives us friends. We can love and help our friends.

God Gives Me Friends

Do

When playing with children, sing "Who is my friend?" to the tune of "God Is So Good" while pretending to look around the room. Then sing song again using the name of a child: "Ellie is my friend."

Say

I'm glad God gives us friends.

God gives us friends to play with. God gives us friends to help us. We can help our friends, too.

Thank You, God, for the friends who are here today: Ellie, Alex and Jordan.

Pictures and Books

Here Are My Friends

Collect

Photo of each child placed in a child-safe photo album

Do

Look at the photo album with a child. Name each child you see and describe what the child is doing in the photo.

Say

Hailey, let's find your picture in this book. Look, there is your friend Sophie.

God gives us so many friends. Friends love each other.

Tip

Keep a camera available to take pictures of the children in your nursery. (Ask parents' permission to photograph and display pictures in an album to be kept in the nursery.)

Friends Help Each Other

Collect

August Poster from *Nursery Posters*

Do

Display the photo at child's eye level. Talk about the photo, describing the way in which the children are helping each other.

Say

I see two children playing with a toy. They are sharing. These children are friends.

God gives you friends, too. Luis and Marcos are here today. They are friends. I'm glad God gives us friends.

Pretend Play

Smile!

Collect

Toy camera and/or a discarded child-safe camera

Do

Use the camera to take a picture of one or more children, saying "Smile!" Let a child use the camera, too. Say the names of the children who are being "photographed."

Say

I see lots of friends in this room. I'm taking a picture of Samantha! Can you smile for the camera, Samantha?

We're glad to be together with our friends today. God gives us friends. Friends love and help each other.

Dolly and Me

Collect

Several dolls
Play dishes and cups
Several other items in your room (picture books, toys, etc.)

Do

Pretend to talk to a doll: "Hi, will you be my friend? Let's have a snack." Then give another doll to a child. Let the child help you pretend to serve the dolls a snack on play dishes.

Say

Lydia, let's give our friends something good to eat. Friends like to play together. Friends like to help each other.

God gives us friends. Thank You, God, for our friends.

Quiet Play

Twos

Collect

Variety of toys—two similar of each (balls, dolls, toy cars, blocks, etc.)

Do

Show a toddler two similar items. Describe the items and set them on the floor. Show and describe several other pairs of items.

When several of the pairs are on the floor, ask, "Can you give me the two cars?" If the child is able to do this, acknowledge his or her efforts. If the child is not yet ready to do this, point to the cars yourself.

Continue to ask the child for the other pairs as long as he or she is interested.

Say

I'm glad to play with you. Friends play with each other and friends help each other. God gives us friends.

Shapes for Me and You

Collect

Variety of matching geometric shapes (square, circle, triangle) cut from felt
Flannel board

Do

Put shapes on flannel board or on the floor. Let a child play with the shapes by placing them on and removing them from a flannel board.

When the child picks up a shape, identify the shape. Pick up a matching shape and say its name. Hand your shape to the child.

Repeat activity several times with different shapes.

Say

Vanessa, you're my friend. Friends like to play together. I'm so glad God gave me a friend like you.

We have lots of friends to play with. I see Maria. I see Jerome. We can love our friends and help them.

Tip

Take turns with a child in putting the shapes on the flannel board. Your participation can make the activity last longer.